Speaking Secrets of the Masters

**The Personal Techniques Used by
22 Of The World's Top Professional Speakers**

by the members of Speakers Roundtable

First Edition 1995
EXECUTIVE BOOKS
Life Management Services, Inc.
Mechanicsburg, PA

Printed in the United States of America
ISBN 0-937539-22-8

Dedicated to

IRA HAYES, CPAE

Ambassador of Enthusiasm

April 25, 1921 - April 26, 1995

"A service of Thanksgiving to almighty God for the life and witness of Ira Hayes." This was the opening sentence for Ira's memorial services which expresses the hearts of the millions who heard him. Ira never gave a speech; he gave himself. He preached what he practiced at N.C.R. for thirty-two years and then for his second career, the practiced what he preached as he became one of America's Master Speakers.

Ira didn't have to act enthusiastic; Ira was enthusiasm from the tip of his toes to the top of his head. His spirit of living and giving made him hero, role model and mentor to millions. His books, film, videos and cassettes will continue to educate, motivate and challenge his listeners forever.

Only a great God would make a man and a life like Ira Hayes. He was a husband, father, salesman, executive, trainer, teacher, author, humorist and servant. Thank you, God, for giving us Ira Hayes and thank you, Ira, for giving us you.

Foreword

Take a moment to reflect on some of the most influential and revered people throughout history: Abraham Lincoln, Winston Churchill, Elanor Roosevelt, John F. Kennedy, Martin Luthur King, Jr...the list goes on. All had at least one thing in common: They could speak with eloquence in front of a group–and often in front of a nation and the world. In particular, they expressed their ideas so that people not only heard and understood, but also acted upon their call to duty.

Your calling as a public speaker is to constantly strive to improve upon your skills so that you not only communicate with your listeners but also connect with them. With that goal in mind, you have come to a worthwhile and valuable source. The range of expertise contained within these pages represents some of the top talent in the field of public speaking. Take these tips, learn from them, and use them to make your presentations the best they can be. The rewards that follow will amaze you.

Unfortunately, many a potential spellbinder remains glued to his seat, daunted by the prospect of facing an audience. But the good news is that jittery nerves, fear of failure, and the procrastination often associated with writing and giving a speech can be relieved by this book, Speaking Secrets Of The Masters. For the inexperienced public speaker, this indispensable guide will calm nerves and strengthen spirits as it explains how to assess an audience and prepare and deliver a memorable message. Seasoned orators will also benefit by the platform-tested tips included in this anthology.

As Executive Director of the world's leading organization devoted to public speaking and leadership training, I have witnessed firsthand the transformation of formerly tongue-tied and nervous speakers into polished and confident orators. The benefits that accompany such a transformation are well worth the time and effort invested.

Many employers recognize the value of strong communication skills and often consider them the most important qualification for the job applicants. Indeed, the ability to speak confidently is one of the most marketable skills we can acquire, as companies continually seek individuals who can sell products, present proposals, report findings, and relate ideas more effectively than their competitors.

It is no coincidence that 50 percent of Toastmasters Clubs are in-house corporate groups that meet at such major corporate groups that meet at such major companies as McDonnell Douglas, Dow Chemical, and American Airlines. We are also represented in government agencies such as NASA, the Department of Justice, and the Senate.

At no other time is the need for effective communication more important than when we speak to a group of people, whether it be colleagues, clients, or conference-goers. In our fast-paced, complex society, one seemingly ruled by computers and technology, effective verbal communication is vital. We need men and women who can inform, persuade, entertain, motivate, and inspire.

So if you want to become a dynamic speaker, I urge you to do two things: One, read this book. Two, get on your feet and practice what you've learned. Don't worry if you don't sound like a "pro" at the first attempt. Stay with it, and before long, you'll be in command of a skill that can change your life. Good luck!

Terrence J. McCann
Executive Director
Toastmasters International

Speaking Secrets of the Masters

Preface

"If you would be successful, study those who are already successful." This timeless wisdom has been passed along in speeches since the beginning of civilization. As Cavett Robert, founder of the National Speakers Association says, "Learning from the school of hard knocks is very informing, but the tuition is too high! We should learn from other people's experience."

The following pages are filled with the collected wisdom of 22 of the most popular and successful professional speakers of this century, the members of Speakers Roundtable. Each of them has earned several million dollars in speaking fees, delivered several thousand presentations, and spoken to audiences around the world.

Speakers Roundtable was formed in the 1960's as a way for the handful of people who traveled the speaking circuit to support and advance each other. Its members have been some of the greatest speakers of the era. Today, it is a special network of just 22 individuals whose primary career focus has been professional speaking. They meet twice each year to sharpen their skills and deepen their friendships.

As you read these pages and gain ideas and insights from these speakers, please take the point of view that you are with them in person. Consider what you would ask each of them, how their answers would differ, and in what ways their answers would be the same. What can you learn from that?

Each of the speakers who contributed to this book is different, with a vastly different background, speaking style, and philosophy toward life. You will no doubt identify strongly with certain speakers and less strongly with others. But all of them have something profound to teach you. Open your mind to what they have to share, then watch new doors of opportunity open for you.

How To Increase Your True Speaking Power

Cavett Robert, CSP, CPAE
1620 W. Glendale Avenue, #9
Phoenix, AZ 85021
602-864-1880

Although I subscribe to the theory that honest arrogance is better than insincere humility, I say in all sincerity that I have every reason to present these ideas in deep humility. I've stolen ideas and stories with a wild sense of abandon, In fact, the more I admire a person, the more of his or her material will be found in this chapter. My only excuse is that I steal only from the best. If there is a blue book of Who's Who of Thieves, I boast that I'm entitled to a listing.

For years I've heard it said that if I steal only one idea, it is plagiarism. I'm a thief! If, however, I steal many ideas, it is education. I'm engaged in research. I hope the multiplicity of my thievery will vindicate me by putting me in this second category.

Furthermore, I'm told that if my pursuits lead me into matters which are interesting to me alone, I possess great intellectual curiosity and am pursuing scientific enquiry. However, if these matters are of interest to everyone, I'm just plain nosy. At the risk of being nosey, I've sought to embody in this chapter the distilled experience of many people in the speaking field. I write the above, not by way of apology, not by way of boastfulness, but by way of clarification. Success needs no explanation. Failure permits no alibi.

The greatest success tool

Let's start out this chapter on speaking with a major premise so articulately expressed throughout all speaking courses of any note, that one of the greatest tools for success in any line of endeavor is the ability to stand on our feet confidently, speak articulately, and express our thoughts in the logical order of their sequence. This is often the difference between rising to success and floundering in mediocrity.

We might express the idea another way. Any person who cannot speak articulately and express his or her thoughts well is handicapped in accomplishing his or her life goals. Both you and I have heard it said that a person who *doesn't* read is no better off than a person who can't read. We can say the same about communication. People who can't communicate their ideas and knowledge are no better off than those people who do not possess these ideas and that knowledge. It's so strange that many people boast of their ability to speak one-to-one, nose-to-nose, toes-to-toes, people who think that they are actually glib in personal conversation. Yet, when these same people are faced with more than one person, they die, communication-wise. Rigor mortis sets in. They can't lead a group in silent prayer.

Actually, there's a divine potentiality within every one of us. The world needs it and is waiting for it. One of the greatest tragedies in life is the waste of human resources. Too many people die today with their music still within them, never having released their imprisoned splendor.

The significance of "want"

Let's begin this chapter with a vital question: Do you really want to learn to speak?

I stress the word "want" advisedly. Because, unless a person definitely and sincerely wants to master the art of conveying his ideas and thoughts in a persuasive manner, he should close this book at this moment. Furthermore, the desire must be deep enough and compulsive enough to cause him or her to follow certain suggestions and instructions contained in these chapters. We make no promise that learning to speak is an easy task that can be accomplished overnight. We do promise, however, that if you will stay with us through the entire book and devote yourself to principles contained herein, you will be amazed at the progress you can make!

In no phase of your life are there so many undeclared dividends, so much unrealized potential, as there are in the field of good communication, whether it be communication to five people or five thousand. I repeat once again: You must *want* to become a better speaker.

Think about this. At this moment, you and I have everything in life that we really want, or at least we are acquiring it so fast that it will soon be ours. Now wait. Let me make myself clear. I didn't say we have everything in life that we wish for, dream about, or stand by the revolving door of life hoping to go through on somebody else's push. I said that we have everything in life we *really* want, because if we really want something, that compulsive desire will be powerful enough and strong enough to generate all the other qualities necessary for accomplishment of our desires. In this regard, there can be no compromise with mediocrity. We must expend the effort.

I say again that it is not easy. We have instant coffee, instant tea, but there is no quickie when it comes to mastering the art of communicating with any group, however small or however large. Please remember this: Mastering the art of speaking is not an overnight project. It takes time. We can't throw an egg into the barnyard and expect it to crow tomorrow.

I once had an uncle who was always sitting around daydreaming, always saying what he planned to do when his ship comes in. Hell! He never sent one out! That's the only sure way of missing the boat.

Let me emphasize this point with a personal illustration. When I was a kid, Houdini, the greatest magician of the time, came to Starkville, Mississippi, under the auspices of the Red Path Chatauqua. He asked for some kid to come to the stage and help him with the rabbit trick. I was a ham then, just as I suppose I am now, and I rushed to the stage. Afterward, as a reward, he gave me a little book on amateur magic, which I have even to this day. There's a passage in that book which I feel is a spark of genius. It refers to the rabbit trick, but in reality, it encompasses a great element of success. Houdini said, "There is no trick to getting the rabbit out of the hat. The real trick is getting him in there in the first place."

No tricks

We can say the same thing about mastering the art of speaking. There is no trick in learning to speak courageously, confidently, and persuasively. The real trick is in ever getting a person to embrace the sincere desire, that deep compulsion *within himself*, to speak. Yes, getting it within himself. When this is once accomplished, then success in speaking will follow in natural sequence.

We must take the time and effort to train ourselves to be good speakers. There is no shortcut. I repeat again and again and again, it is not an easy path. It's a pilgrim's journey. The only thing I can assure you is that if you stay with it, you will grow strong in the journey. Just as the law of gravity causes the apple to fall to the ground, just as the law of growth causes the acorn to become the oak, so the law of hard work and constant effort can surely make you a good speaker.

Let's start out on the basis that we are willing to work hard over a long period of time, with the goal in mind of not just learning to make a good speech, but rather of becoming a good speaker. This is the surest approach to success in the field of speaking.

Just as water cannot rise above its source, we cannot accomplish anything except that which we are. The book cannot be any greater than the writer, the picture no greater than the painter, the speech no better than the speaker. I repeat: We cannot accomplish anything any greater than ourselves. Many people are more concerned with what they have accomplished and what they have, rather than in what they are.

Do you remember the old Chinese proverb, "Give a man a fish and he will eat for a day; teach him to fish and you've satisfied his hunger for life"? I am hopeful that in some measure, this book on speaking can open doors of opportunity for you, doors which you did not even know existed.

It has been said that words are the fingers that mold the mind of man. Words are magic. The person who masters the art of using them properly is the magician. The great Carl Winters, second president of our National Speakers Association, expressed the idea so beautifully by the magic of the spoken word. He said, "We tip men's minds out of bed, stab their spirits awake, and set them on the forward march for a better personal, professional, and business life. All who hear us can be sent out a little wiser, walking a little taller, and living and saying it a little better. We have a matchless opportunity to affect the quality of life at this challenging point in time."

I love that statement of Carl's. Furthermore, I'm sure we all realize that the process of persuasion is the keystone in the arch upon which all civilization rests. It accounts for our orderly system of living. If this were not true, man would still be carrying the ancient club in order to get by physical force the necessities of life. At one time, brute force was the only method of satisfying needs and wants. Under these uncivilized conditions, all of life was simply a struggle for survival, and it belonged only to the fittest, the so-called "giants" of that day.

We have progressed far from the days of the caveman. To some extent, the principle known as "survival of the fittest" affects our civilization even in modern times. But those who survive today, those who have the greatest share of the rewards of life, are not necessarily people of physical prowess. They are individuals who have learned the art of persuading others to think and act as the speaker desires. It is an art which each of us can develop, if only we are willing to study certain basic principles and put them to use. When we have once mastered these principles, I think we can safely say that then we are a success. Maybe we shall have to wait for the fruits of success, but I say we are already wealthy. And some day, we will have money to prove it.

Persuasion, a lifelong effort

To live successfully, we must be able to sell our ideas to others. We are engaged in the effort of persuasion from the moment we are born until we draw our final breath.

No one is more gifted in this quality than a tiny baby. He persuades us to feed him or change him by crying. When he wants to be picked up and loved, he smiles and coos. What a sales pitch! Who can resist?

The little boy sells his teacher with an apple. The young blade swept up by the first blush of love presents his case to his sweetheart with candy or flowers. Years ago, a man would wait on his proposal of marriage for days, even weeks. It was the most important sale of his life. I'm afraid this sale is often a little more casual today, but it is still a vital sale, regardless of who sells whom.

What man has not spent sleepless nights mentally rehearsing his approach to the boss in an effort to persuade him that a salary raise is in order? The doctor has to persuade his patients. The lawyer has to persuade the jury. The pastor must persuade his congregation. As someone has said, "When it's foggy in the pulpit, it's blamed cloudy in the pew." As parents, we give major importance to focusing all of our powers on instilling character in our children and on teaching them right living. Can you think of anyone who is exempt from the necessity of learning how to cause others to think and feel and act as we desire? We don't all use the same approach. Our desired results are not the same. But everyone in essence wants to master the art, through good speaking methods, of causing the other person to do what we want them to do.

Yes, we know that when a person has learned to communicate to this extent, by acquiring good speaking habits, he is then a *creator* of circumstances, not a creature of circumstances. Things don't happen to him. He happens to things. He's the cause, not the result. People are his opportunity, not his frustration.

I'm sure that you agree with me that the process of persuading people to think and act as we desire is the very essence of our existence. It is the balance wheel that gives stability, not only to our entire economic system, but to life itself. And yet, in spite of the fact that the extent to which we cause others to think, believe, and act as we desire affects our lives more than any other single quality that we possess. Only a few of us give this matter any great amount of steady consideration.

I suppose that one of the disenchanting experiences of this life is that we often enter into a business, industry, or profession, conceiving it in all of its beauty and majesty. It's an exciting journey in the pursuit of our dreams, with a pot of gold at the end of the rainbow. But then too soon, we are shocked to realize that somewhere between the little town of reality in which we live and the great city of our dreams and our aspirations, out in the blue yonder, there is a little hamlet called compromise. Unfortunately, that is where many of us spend the rest of our lives.

We don't find these towns on any map. They are not listed in any census report. But they are as much a part of your life and mine as the town in which we live, pay taxes, and vote. And how close our little town of compromise is located to the great city of our dreams and ambitions depends, more than anything else, on how well we master the art—I repeat—of standing on our feet courageously, speaking understandably, and presenting our thoughts in the logical order of their sequence.

Your future depends on today

Just for emphasis, let me put it another way. If you could reach through an imaginary door and take the hand of the person you will be five years from today, and take your alter ego over into a corner for a little intimate fireside chat, what do you think your conversation would be? Would you even want the privilege? Do you think you would have the courage to go through with the experience? Would this person put his arms about you and thank you for taking the time and expending the effort to learn through steady and constant practice to communicate your ideas to others through effective speaking? Would he thank you for putting importance on learning to express your ideas professionally? Or would you have to drop your eyes, dig your toe, twist your button, and try to explain to him why you let him down? Would you be required to apologize to him by confessing that you were so busy, in the confused affairs of the moment, that you just didn't have time to devote to becoming effective in the art of speaking?

Well, I've got news for you. Strange as it may seem, you are going to meet this person many times in the future. You can't avoid him, you can't evade him, you can't escape him. Your eyes will meet his in the mirror each morning. You'll break bread three times a day with him. You even must sleep with the rascal at night. Now, whether that person thanks you or criticizes you could well depend upon how conscientiously and how enthusiastically you work to master the principles in this book. I repeat, you've got to _want_ to.

To grow, we must have the gift of dissatisfaction. We must want circumstances to be better than they are now. If we are completely satisfied with our present state in life and with everything that surrounds us, the pilgrimage has ended for us, and we've already settled in our little city of compromise. We're bogged down in the quicksands of complacency, lost in the sterile valleys of inertia, and frozen in the ices of status quo. It is only through divine discontent that we keep moving forward.

Remember, you gotta wanta. Needs are not enough. Wants are

the magic ingredient. Wants alone—not needs—bring out the best in us. We are not, and probably never will be, a needy people. Needs are too basic and logical, and they push us only while we are in the realm of desperation. Wants are emotional, inspirational, and sentimental. They lift us to new levels of accomplishment. If it were not true that wants have a greater moving power than needs, then why are there more television sets in this country than there are bathtubs?

If we want certain things in life badly enough, we automatically draw upon those resources within us and convert them to productivity. We might have needed certain things for a long time, but until we finally begin to want them, we shall certainly never get them unless by accident. Many people who merely need things sit idly by and dream of the joys they will experience when their dream ship comes in. This is the only sure way of missing the boat. But the man who really and truly wants something knows the ship of opportunity has already docked for him and is only waiting for him to unload his priceless cargo.

Opportunity is waiting

I once felt that the most tragic man was the ambitious man who lacked opportunity. Now I am firmly convinced that this is really not true. The real catastrophe is the great opportunities of this wonderful world without men and women of ambition and visions who want to embrace them.

We only have to look around us to see people groveling in economic poverty while Opportunity eagerly stretches out her arms to us. As we open our eyes each morning, she forgets and forgives any neglect of the past. Each night we burn the records of the day; at sunrise, every soul is born again. In our pilgrimage of life toward the great city of our dreams and ambitions, first of all, let's not be satisfied to let the great reservoirs within us go untapped. Let's not permit the great sleeping forces within us to remain asleep. If we don't already have the gifts of dissatisfaction and divine discontent, let's develop these qualities.

You might say, "Why shout the obvious? Of course, I'm inter-ested in becoming a better speaker! Why would I be reading this book if I had not already made up my mind?"

Don't deal in vague generalities. Be specific. Nothing clutters up the landscape of understanding so much as generalities. Specifics alone give a directional compass to life.

Perhaps you are saying, "Tell me in detail just what I should do. I'm prepared to start right now. I want to be a good speaker." If this is your attitude, I'm happy for you. I congratulate you. I say from the bottom of my heart that my fellow members of Speakers Roundtable and I want to help you. And that is our goal in this book. So, let's get started.

Cavett Robert is founder of the National Speakers Association. When he retired from his law practice, he started what became an illustrious speaking career. He has received the coveted Golden Gavel Award, presented annually by Toastmasters International to only one speaker recognized as the nation's outstanding speaker in the field of leadership and communication. From a canvass of more than 10,000 associations, meeting planners, and corporations, Cavett was selected by United Airlines and International Speakers Network as Speaker of the Year. He was presented with the Speakers Hall of Fame Award by Sales and Marketing Executives International. Today, the National Speakers Association's most coveted award, presented annually to only one speaker, is entitled "The Cavett."

A One Minute Course In Public Speaking

Ken Blanchard, Ph.D., CPAE
Blanchard Training
  and Development, Inc.
125 State Place
Escondido, CA 92029
619-489-5005
800-728-6000
Fax 619-489-1332

My speaking career started when I was 12 years old. I had been nominated for president of my seventh grade class in New Rochelle, New York, and needed to make a campaign speech in front of my class at a special assembly. I was nervous, to say the least, but my father settled me down. He was a commander in the Navy and was continually asked to speak at various Naval affairs. He told me, "Start off with a joke. Get everyone laughing, and then you've got them in the palm of your hand."

That sounded easy. So after being introduced and receiving applause from students and teachers, I stood up and said, "As the cow said to the farmer when the milking machine broke down, 'Thanks for that warm hand!'"

The band teacher, Harry Haigh, was sitting in the front row, and for some reason my joke hit his funny bone. He roared. A few others followed suit, and finally everyone was laughing. With that beginning, I relaxed and gave my pitch. And, I won the election.

That advice I received from my father was the first and last speaking advice I ever got until I took a public speaking course as a student at Cornell University. That was one of the best courses I ever took, and I will always remember John Wilson, our instructor. He was so excited about all of us becoming good speakers that his enthusiasm became infectious. In fact, I think a public speaking course should be required of all high school and college students.

If I were going to teach that course, I would emphasize four secrets—secrets that are at the core of what has made me a successful speaker.

Secret #1: Controlling nervousness

As I mentioned in the beginning, one of the best ways to overcome nervousness is to tell an opening joke. If you can get people laughing, then you can relax and will be able to deliver your message better.

If that doesn't do the trick, I once got some fabulous advice from Dorothy Sarnoff, president of Speech Dynamics and one of the great speaking coaches in this country. Dorothy and I were speakers together at a Young Presidents' Organization (YPO) conference. She also helped prepare me for television appearances when *The One Minute Manager*® was first published.

When people are nervous before beginning to speak, Dorothy tells them to say over and over again the following:

> I'm glad I'm here.
> I'm glad you're here.
> I know what I know.
> And I care about you.

I've seen Dorothy work with people who are so nervous that they could hardly speak. But after saying that statement over and over again, they started to relax.

Dorothy not only combined a mantra exercise that is good for

meditation (the ultimate in relaxation), but the words she suggested you repeat have real meaning in terms of speaking. Think
about them!

I'm glad I'm here. Sometimes you might not be glad you are
there, but you must get yourself into the mind-set that you are
very happy to be there speaking before this group.

I'm glad you're here. Without an audience, you won't have
much of a chance to be a successful speaker. So you should be
glad that they are there with you.

I know what I know. This is so important. Don't try to be an
expert in an area that is not your field. When you are speaking,
stick to what you know. And finally:

I care about you. Without caring about your audience, you
are in big trouble from the start. It is your caring that will really
come across and make your message come alive.

So, humor and Dorothy Sarnoff's mantra can help you in
terms of nervousness.

Secret #2: The power of visualization

All great athletes talk about the power of visualization. They
usually see themselves successfully finishing the race before they
even start. They see themselves jumping over the bar as they're
starting towards it.

When I speak to a group, the first thing I see in my mind
before I get on my feet is the audience leaping to their feet and
giving me a standing ovation, then turning to each other and saying things like, "That was one of the best speeches I ever heard"
or, "Wasn't he fabulous!" I find that when I see the end result
ahead of time, I can relax and get myself in an easy mind-set to
move toward that direction. Why? Because I feel that the job is
already done. I've achieved my goal. Now I can concentrate on
being the best. Visualizing the results before you begin is very
powerful.

Secret #3: You are the message

A number of years ago, I asked Dorothy Jongeward, co-author of the best-selling book *Born To Win*, to make a presentation for one of my clients. Dorothy is one of the outstanding teachers in the field of transactional analysis. As I was driving Dorothy back to the airport, I said to her, "Dorothy, I couldn't have gotten anybody better in the country to teach transactional analysis than you."

"Yes, you could have," Dorothy replied, "but you couldn't have gotten anyone to do Dorothy Jongeward as well. You see, transactional analysis is the way I have decided to share myself."

What Dorothy said to me that day has had a powerful impact on me ever since. It made me realize that you, as the speaker, are really the message. Your speech is the way you have decided to share yourself. Don't get so overloaded in content that the real you doesn't come out in your message. Always remember this: Whenever you are speaking, whatever you are saying, *you* are the message.

I'll never forget a few summers ago when John Denver asked me to come and speak to his Windstar Conference in Aspen, Colorado. My wife Margie and I got there on Thursday night and sat in on everyone's sessions on Friday. They had the most incredible people at that conference that I have ever met. For example, they had people who had been nominated for "giraffe awards." These are people who had stuck their necks out for mankind. Everyone was committed to making the world a better place.

Friday's conference ended with John Denver and the most popular singer in Russia at the time singing together. When they had first met, the only English that the Russian singer knew was Beatles songs. Singing some of those songs had started their wonderful relationship. For this concert, they had written several songs together about the cruelty and inhumanity in the world. Their songs always ended with an uplifting message about how the world could be a better place.

I was scheduled to speak the next morning. At 4:00 a.m., I was up wandering around the room. When Margie heard me stirring, she woke up too. "What's going on?" she asked.

I replied, "What can I possibly talk to these people about? This is the first group I have ever been with that I honestly feel inadequate. I feel like I'm not doing enough. These people are all reaching out almost every day trying to help make the world a better place."

Margie, in her infinite wisdom, laughed and said, "Just talk about yourself. That's all you know about anyway. Tell them exactly what you just told me and how this conference is impacting you. By the time you've done that, you'll be ready to share some insights that might help them."

Margie was so right. In sharing what was happening to me, I was able to relate to the audience, and then was amazed how things came to me that were important to share. *You* are the message.

Secret #4: Inspire people, don't just share information

I was once asked to give a speech at the regional NSA meeting in San Diego about my speaking approach. They wanted me to tell others how I give a speech. In contemplating that assignment, I realized that I do have a format.

First, I give people a concept that could help them be a better manager, teacher, coach, or parent. Next, I tell a story that relates to that concept. I get people laughing. Finally, I zero in on audience members as human beings, trying to make my point in such a way that it triggers an emotional reaction for each person. I want them to identify with what I am saying. It might even inspire them to take some new action.

Let me give you an example. Of all the concepts that I have taught over the years, the most important is about "catching people doing things right." There is little doubt in my mind that the key to developing people is to catch them doing something right and praising them for their performance. And there are many ways you can praise someone. Bob Nelson, who serves as vice president of product development for our company, wrote the best-selling book, *1001 Ways to Reward Employees* (Workman, 1994). Bob's book is filled with ideas about how you can praise employees for doing things right. The minute you begin talking about catching someone doing things right, praising that person and letting him or her know you noticed their good performance, that person's attention perks up.

After I talk to an audience about praising in a general sense, I warn people not to wait for exactly the right behavior to praise others—because they could be waiting forever! In the beginning, when people are learning something and are not top performers yet, you have to praise progress.

I ask my audience to imagine trying to teach a child how to talk. You decide you want her to say, "Give me a glass of water, please." If she has never spoken before and you wait for that full sentence before you give the child a sip of water, what have you got? A dead, dehydrated kid, that's what! So what do you do? You have to praise progress.

First, you zero in on water. Repeat it over and over again. Finally, the child will respond with something like "loller." When that happens, hug and kiss the kid. Call grandmother and get the child on the phone so she can say, "Loller, loller, loller." While that's not "water," it's not bad. After a while, you will only accept "water." Why? Because you don't want your child going into a restaurant at 21 years of age and asking for a glass of "loller." So praising progress helps people move towards desired performance.

Is praising important in relationships other than with our children? You better believe it. So now I get my audience to think about other applications for the concept.

Have you ever seen a couple in a restaurant in love? While one is talking, what is the other one doing? He or she is smiling, listening, and pawing. On the other hand, have you ever seen a married couple in a restaurant? They look like they couldn't get anyone else to eat with them. They have nothing to say.

Margie and I were at a French restaurant not long ago, where we spent three and one-half hours enjoying a marvelous meal and the elegant atmosphere. On one side of us was a couple in love. I don't think they cared if the meal ever came. On the other side was a couple that obviously had been married for a while. In three and one-half hours, I don't think they said four sentences to each other. He finally said, "How's your meat?" "Okay," was the reply. "How's yours?" I said to Margie, "That marriage is dead. Nobody buried it."

How do you get from hanging onto someone's every word to having nothing to say? It's the frequency with which you catch each other doing things right.

Have you ever heard the expression, "Love is blind"? What does that mean? In the beginning, you only see the good qualities in the other person. Then what happens after you get married or move in with the person? Pretty soon you start noticing everything that is wrong. You start to think things to yourself like, "I didn't know anything about that." Or, "You gotta be kidding me." Or, "I can't believe it!" The final demise of a love relationship is when you do something right but you get yelled at for not doing it right enough. "You should have done it on Wednesday." "You had to ask me!"

The key to keeping relationships going is to constantly catch each other doing things right, and accent the positive. When you accent the positive, you have deposits in your human relationship bank with that person. Now, if he or she does something wrong, you can point it out without devastating the relationship. Unfortunately, most relationships deteriorate to the point that you focus on catching the other person doing things wrong.

The example I've just presented demonstrates how I try to present a concept in human terms and involve the audience in a way that it stirs an emotional reaction in each person. I try to relate the concept to something that is present in the lives of every audience member so they can feel the power of the concept. Remember that your job as a speaker is to inspire and change people's behavior, not just share information.

The privilege of sharing

One final thought. Never adopt the attitude expressed by this thought: "I've got to give another speech tonight." You don't have to give another speech tonight or any time. You have the privilege of giving another speech. You get to share who you are. You get to help people with their lives. What a wonderful opportunity.

Ken Blanchard, co-author of *The One Minute Manager®*, is an internationally-known author, educator, consultant, and speaker. In addition to being named CPAE (the National Speakers Association's highest honor) in 1992, Ken received the Golden Gavel from Toastmasters International in 1991. As co-founder with his wife Marjorie of Blanchard Training and Development, Inc., Blanchard considers himself the Chief Spiritual Officer of his company. His mission in life is "to be a loving teacher and example of simple truths that help himself and others to awaken the presence of God in our lives." His most recent best-selling book, *Everyone's A Coach*, was co-authored with Don Shula, head coach of the Miami Dolphins and the "winningest" coach in National Football League history.

Speaking Soul To Soul 3

Charlie Plumb
1200 N. San Marcos Road
Santa Barbara, CA 93111
805-683-1969
Fax 805-683-4142

I've always believed effective communication is not so much from voice box to eardrum as it is from soul to soul. Whether your purpose is to close the big sale by making a highly convincing, one-on-one presentation or to deliver a rousing State of the Union address to hundreds of millions of people, you will be wise to put aside your "voice box to eardrum" concerns of technical communication and examine what's in the soul of your listener and how best to transfer your emotional fervor to that soul.

If this approach sounds simplistic or even preachy to you, I suggest you scan your memory to recall the greatest speeches you've ever heard.

"Ask not what your country can do for you" and "I have a dream" are great examples of the value of the emotional factor in a soul-to-soul speech. Even in presentations demanding highly technical material, your facts will be better digested and longer remembered if your words touch the heart before they stimulate the mind.

The first question to ask yourself on the journey to creating and delivering soul-to-soul presentations is, "What's really going on in the depth of the soul of my audience? What are the joys, what are the fears, what stimulates, what depresses the people who will hear my message? And, how do I go about finding this information? Once I have found it, how do I pluck the strings of this magical harp to communicate harmony that moves the heart?"

Look to your audience

Consider first the recipient of your message, which could be an audience of one or one thousand. Each audience has a personal character of its own.

What motivates this audience as a group? What words do they all know that no one else knows? What names, places, or dates would be famous only to them? What are their secrets? Specifically, what would cause this audience to laugh and what would cause them to cry? Where is this audience's soul?

"Hold everything!" you may want to shout. "That sounds like work, and I'm not even getting paid for this!" Well, it can be as much work or as much fun as you make it. The amazing thing is the ROI (that's Return-On-Investment for non-financial types). With as little as 15 minutes spent scanning a company brochure or a local newspaper, and another 15 minutes asking some basic questions to a "typical" audience member, you can unlock the communications link that makes you look like William Jennings Bryant.

To explain this more specifically, let me select a not-so-typical audience. I'll call my audience the Rabbit Ears, Montana, Downtown Rotary Club. Now let me walk though my standard preparation steps for you.

Reading the Rotary

To begin with, I would probably find that a copy of the *Rabbit Ears Gazette*, the Rotary newsletter, and a packet furnished by the Rabbit Ears Chamber of Commerce would provide an invaluable window to the soul of this community.

Q. What motivates this audience?

A. As a community, these citizens of Montana are motivated by a sense of rugged individualism, of wide-open spaces and big blue sky. (It says so in all their tourism brochures.) They are turned off by fast-talkin' city slickers and politicians.

As are all Rotary Clubs, this one is motivated by service—the giving of oneself, asking nothing in return. They are motivated by connections and communications, thus the Rotary Wheel. As most are business professionals, they are motivated by a healthy economy, basic community wellness, and—of course—free enterprise and the profit potential it brings.

Q. What specific words do they use that no one else knows?

A. This takes a little research, but thumbing through the local newspaper, Chamber of Commerce brochures, and a phone call to the "local" might reveal to you that Bugsy's Bar and Grill is *the* place to be seen, and the new Town and Country Mall is facing a challenge by the E.P.A. over their heating system. Within the typical Rotary propaganda, you'll find "service above self," "polio plus," "Paul Harris," and other words and phrases repeated.

Q. What makes them cry?

A. The increased rate of teen suicide in Rabbit Ears, Montana. The closing of the local mine and subsequent loss of 200 jobs. The recent scandal involving the pastor of the largest church in town and his secretary.

Q. What brings them joy?

A. Their past president has just been elected to serve as Mayor of the city. The local high school has been all-conference basketball champs for three straight years.

As you can see, finding the soul of this heterogeneous group we call an "audience" requires some research. But I can guarantee the research will pay great dividends in terms of drawing the communication line straight to the heart of your audience.

Each group you address, be it tough salespeople or bored school kids, is made up of individuals. And each individual has his or her own soul that contributes in various ways and to various degrees to the heart of the audience. The smaller the number of an audience, the more diligently the speaker should search for the individual soul.

It's all a matter of probabilities. To speak to a specific individual in a crowd of 1,000 would exclude (and perhaps frustrate) the other 999, unless the majority of the audience relates closely to the specific individual you have singled out. So the trick is to be general enough to reach the majority of the audience, and yet so specific that each person in the room feels you are talking directly to him or her. A specific question you might pose to that typical individual is the following:

Q. Is the soul of this person steeped in areas of religious, ethnic, racial, or gender identity? What are his or her political leanings—liberal or conservative? Democrat or Republican?

Once the soul is found, the speaker needs to find the pathway to that soul. This, of course, can be done through a number of techniques and tools—gestures, expressions, slides, charts, overheads, lights, etc. But the catalyst that holds it all together in any presentation are the *words* that you use. Words that reach out and touch the inner feelings of the audience are the jewels that transfer emotion from soul to soul.

Word choice can be a risky business, of course. To mispronounce a familiar name or to err when describing some intimate association (in an area where you haven't done your homework) can destroy your credibility and thus derail the entire communication connection. Don't let this frighten you. No guts, no glory!

If you've done your homework and checked out your words on a typical audience member or, better yet, in a "focus group" before the final performance, you will have no trouble speaking their language. The truth is, it takes very few "secret words" to convince an audience that you are on their side and even a member of their team.

Well, enough about the heart of the audience. Now let's look a moment at exposing your *own* soul.

Self-revelation

First of all, know this: Whatever your background, whatever your experience, you have credibility first and foremost in speaking from your heart. And the greatest mistake that you can make as a speaker is pretending to be someone or know something that is perceived by an audience as fallacious. "To thine own self be true..." as the Bard said. Consider your belief system and how it developed within you. Think of stories of your childhood or your business life or your day-to-day work. Make them simple, understandable, meaningful, and true.

Admittedly, these stories may seem boring to you. They are likely to be unimportant and insignificant when you first think of them. But, properly selected and told with authenticity, your audience will have just the opposite response. You will be surprised. Personal stories or vignettes told with honesty and enthusiasm can bring more laughter (and tears) to an audience than all the fabrication from all the speech books in the library. So make a list of these stories and jot down the feelings each expresses, along with the specific point you can make by the telling of the story. Try to collect 15 to 20 stories, preferably ones you told your kids, your church group, or your pals on the golf course.

Match feelings and stories

Now for the tricky part. Try to take on the soul of your audience in your mind and match that feeling with one of your personal vignettes. Does the connection make sense? Does it evoke an emotional response? Try to make yourself one with your audience and listen with their eardrums. Scrutinize your stories, asking questions from the character of the audience's soul. Then focus your voice box on those questions.

The next step will take self-discipline, but you can do it. Practice, practice, practice. Start with a mirror or a video camera. Then engage your dog or cat to watch. Next engage a human being—your spouse or a trusted friend. Try a focus group. Each time you practice, add colorful words to your vignette. Soul-to-soul words, words that evoke emotion from the listener—this is what you are seeking. Words that touch the heart!

An endless journey

As you have probably surmised already, creating speeches and presentations that engage the soul of your audience is a never-ending process. You'll catch yourself saying, "This isn't good enough; there isn't enough meat here; I'm not as eloquent as I should be." Don't worry about eloquence. Polish the words enough to get the emotion across.

Once you understand soul-to-soul communicating and get a taste of the response it can evoke, you'll become an enthusiastic student who wants to continue getting better. You'll think of new ways to adapt your stories. You'll develop an ear and a feeling for what will move audiences. You will have begun the endless journey toward becoming a very good speaker. And it is a journey you will come to enjoy.

Other chapters in this book will give you great ideas on the specifics of speech making. Learn them well...but never forget that effective communication begins and ends with the soul-to-soul transfer of emotion between speaker and audience. Have a great trip!

J. Charles "Charlie" Plumb graduated from the Naval Academy at Annapolis. He went on to fly F-4 Phantom jets on 74 successful combat missions over Vietnam. On Mission 75 (only five days before he was to return home), he was shot down, captured, tortured, and imprisoned for the next 2,103 days. Today, Charlie Plumb is one of America's top speakers who tells his story of survival and his philosophy of "winning through adversity" to corporate management and sales teams in this country and around the world. He and his wife Cathy have two children, Joseph and Evelyn.

How To Get
From Fear To Fun

4

Jim Newman, CPAE
The PACE Organization
P.O. Box 1378
Studio City, CA 91614
818-769-5100
Fax 818-769-0000

When you were four years old, you were probably a pretty good public speaker.

It was fun to learn a poem or a joke and then tell it to your family or friends. Then, as a few years went by, some new experiences may have caused you to change your mind. Maybe someone important said, "Be quiet." Or you may have been told, "If you are going to talk, talk, talk, why don't you go outside for awhile?" Perhaps you got the impression that people were laughing at *you* instead of at the joke you told.

So, over a period of time, you may have made up your mind that standing up in front of people and talking wasn't fun at all—in fact, it was downright scary! You were still a great speaker to an audience of one, but if someone asked you to talk to a group, even about your job, your vacation, or your hobby, that was *different*. If it meant getting on your feet and you thought of it as

"giving a speech," you probably declined. You developed a case of "what if" fears:
- What if people laugh?
- What if you forget what you wanted to say?
- What if the group thinks your subject is boring?
- What if you don't begin your talk well?
- What if you talk too long?
- What if they see your knees shaking?
- What if your voice breaks?
- What if you talk too loudly?
- What if you don't talk loudly enough?

You could think of all kinds of reasons for passing up the opportunity, and hardly any reasons for accepting it. And, of course, FEAR was the blockage. Fear that you would perform badly. Fear that people wouldn't admire you—or even like you as well.

And, if someone said, "We're going to sign up for a public speaking course" or "Let's join the Toastmasters," you were probably too busy to join in. Perhaps unconsciously you were doing what you needed to do to be sure that people would not know what a terrible speaker you were.

A learned attitude

Fear of public speaking is not inborn. And it is not universal. It is a learned attitude pattern. And the great news is that *it can be changed!*

Can you think of anything that was once very scary that you now look forward to with joy and eager anticipation? Skiing, perhaps? Skating? Even a bicycle was probably frightening at first, and then it became a source of much fun and freedom. Most people have experienced that change process in a few areas. And, of course, that's what we are eager to do in this chapter—help you convert the *fear* of public speaking into confident, positive *enjoyment* of the activity, which is what we see in top professionals.

There's an old legend that the best actors (or public speakers) are always scared and upset before they "go on." Let me tell you, that's just plain nonsense! And it certainly is nonsense if we are talking about the world's top motivational speakers! Now, that's not to say that a professional speaker is bored or relaxed while being introduced to the audience. Of course not. But let's look at the difference between the *negative* emotion of fear and the *positive* emotion of excitement or eager anticipation that good speakers usually feel as they are about to begin their presentation. One of your most important goals, if you are to become a good public speaker, is to develop *positive emotions* about speaking.

We can express the difference between the negative emotion of fear and the positive emotion of eager anticipation in a simple visual diagram of what tension is all about.

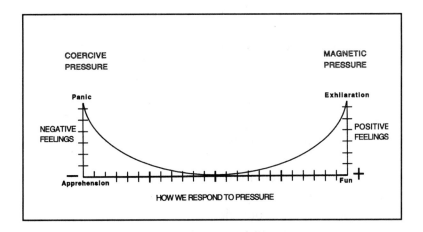

Top professionals in every area *love* pressure! The outstanding brain surgeon is at her or his very best when the operation is critical and the patient is a world-famous celebrity. The best guitarist will perform well for a group of friends, but will excel when on stage at Carnegie Hall, playing for an audience of musical experts. Olympic athletes, top tennis players, or professional golfers *love* the demands of playing against top competitors. The kind of tension they experience is a very positive, enthusiastic, and excited feeling. They see the pressure as a "magnetic" force. They are doing what they are doing because they *want* to be doing it and they know that they have an excellent chance of doing it very well.

At the negative end of this continuum or scale is something called fear. When we see the pressure as a coercive force, it's because we see it as a "have to" instead of a "want to," and we're not sure we can cope. That can be scary. Symptoms are dry mouth, weak knees, loss of memory, upset stomach, cold sweat, and tight throat muscles. Sound familiar? All of these are quite natural physical changes when a person is frightened. And, depending on the situation and how the person is responding to it, there may be just a little apprehension or there may be full-blown panic. So, we really have two scales. The horizontal one ranges from fear to joy. The vertical one represents the amount of the emotion that is being felt.

How, exactly, can you move toward the positive end of this scale? And how can you heighten that positive feeling so that you really do love the idea of standing before a group of people and talking?

Here is a very simple, thoroughly-proven, three-step process for making that change, and you can start working on it right now.

First, get acquainted with the positive emotion a professional speaker feels when making a presentation. Next, crawl into that kind of event and experience exactly how it feels to have that emotion in your system when you're speaking to a group. And, finally, while you are experiencing the speaking activity in your imagination, let yourself feel the joy, the excitement, and the enthusiasm.

Step one

The first step is to get acquainted with just how it feels to love public speaking.

"How can I get acquainted with something that I have never felt?" seems like a very logical question but, fortunately, it is not necessary for you to have experienced the thrill of speaking well to a large group of people in order to understand it and imagine it.

Can you imagine how it would feel to stand on the end of the high diving board and be scared? Most of us will have little or no difficulty with that one! Now, see if you can imagine how it would feel to be a top Olympic high-diving champion. For a champion, standing on the end of that board is challenging, exciting, and rewarding, the culmination of years of preparation, practice, and conditioning. Even if you are not a swimmer, you can let yourself experience that event in your imagination.

Your thoughts might go like this: "If I were an Olympic Gold Medal contender in the high-diving competition, and I'm now standing on the end of the board, ready to do what I do so well, how do I feel?"

You know what it feels like to be all ready to do what you are trained and prepared to do. And, if you want to do so, you can imagine standing on that diving board. Put the two together. You're on the diving board and you feel an eager, excited anticipation.

Okay, let's go back to public speaking. For some, that's even scarier than standing on a high diving board! Think for a moment of the very best public speaker you've ever seen on a platform. It might be an evangelist, a teacher, a professional motivation speaker, or an actor presenting a one-person show. Can you imagine how excited this person feels about the fact that they are about to have a wonderful opportunity to perform, to influence, to teach, to help people expand their horizons?

Try this thought: "If I were (your favorite professional speaker), how would I *feel* when I'm off stage, being introduced, about to have the exciting opportunity to talk about my favorite subject to an audience who is eager to hear what I have to say?" Or, imagine a different situation. An outstanding professional speaker is wrapping up the speech. The audience has been responsive, attentive, and enthusiastic. Now, the speaker closes the talk with one or two very powerful sentences which bring the audience to their feet with a vigorous standing ovation. Can you imagine how the speaker feels?

Step two

Now, let *yourself* experience vividly, in your imagination, the process of speaking well. Experience it as clearly as you possibly can.

Perhaps you are expressing your opinions to a PTA meeting, the local City Council or Town Meeting, or you have been asked to talk to the company's sales team about the new product your department has developed.

Or, imagine that you are speaking to a local service club about some aspect of your job that is new and exciting. The program chairman is introducing you to the audience right now with enthusiasm. As the final words of the introduction come roaring out of the sound system: "And now, please join me in welcoming our speaker, (fill in your name here)!", the audience's applause brings you out onto the stage. Experience this vividly in your imagination. You know you're prepared. You know you have an important message to give to this audience. They are eager to hear what you have to say. You've been in this situation dozens of times and your audience always responds positively.

Right now, you may well be thinking, "But I can't imagine that!"

Yes, you can imagine it. You may not *believe* it, but fortunately that's not required. What's necessary is simply for you to *experience the act of being there and speaking well in your imagination.*

If you know what a polar bear looks like, and you are familiar with the color pink, you can imagine a pink polar bear—even though you've never actually seen one. Imagination is simply putting two or more familiar objects or activities together into a new, unfamiliar form.

You know what it feels like to do something well. And you know how it feels to stand in front of a group of people and speak to them. If you want to do so, you can experience, in your imagination, standing in front of a group of people and expressing yourself very well. Go ahead and try it right now. Imagine the faces of your audience as they give you their attention. Notice how they think about what you are saying, laugh at your humor, and nod their agreement as you proceed.

Step three

The third part of this process is to allow yourself to *feel* the positive emotion that goes with being an outstanding speaker. This is the most important part of the entire system, because the emotions are what control the flow of your skills and knowledge.

The most important difference in the high performer is how he or she feels about what they're doing. People at the top in all walks of life are nearly always being paid for pursuing their hobby. If you're to become a good public speaker, it is absolutely essential that you learn to enjoy speaking. And, when you're really good, it will be because you love it!

Right now, experience in your imagination the excitement, the joy, the enthusiasm, the confidence, the thrill of developing and nurturing a warm rapport with an audience.

You may be inclined to think, "When I'm good, I'll be able to feel some positive emotions." Think again! Turn that around and see how quickly it works. To the degree that you are able to feel the positive emotions, all of the knowledge and skill you have acquired to express yourself well will be available.

Imagined experience is important

Well, there it is. A very simple three-step process. First, get a clear understanding about how the excellent speaker feels about the process. Second, experience speaking well in your imagination. And, finally, allow yourself to feel the positive emotion that a top-notch speaker feels.

In our PACE seminars, we call this technique "constructive imagination." And the fascinating part of it is that all of the top pros in every field do use their imagination to practice their skills, develop confidence, and prepare for new, challenging experiences. You won't find a professional golfer who doesn't play golf in his or her mind a lot. You won't find a surgeon who doesn't perform the operation in the imagination before conducting the surgery. Musicians practice their instruments (or sing) in their imagination. Every top sales professional is constantly practicing the sales presentation, responding to questions, rehearsing trial closes, and all the other skills of selling in the imagination. Before conducting a staff meeting or the meeting of a Board of Directors, the top executive has had that meeting many times in the imagination—thinking about and preparing for all of the questions and the discussion that may occur at that meeting.

None of these people became a high performer entirely in their imagination, of course. The golfer must learn to putt, to hit a long ball well, to get out of the rough or a sand trap, and many other skills. But the best golfers know that the game is about 10 percent aptitude and 90 percent attitude. Public speaking follows just about the same proportions.

If your goal is to become a good public speaker, then you will need to learn the skills: how to use humor, how to organize your presentation, how to tell stories well, how to dramatize ideas, and how to close your presentation with power. You may want to join Toastmasters or the National Speakers Association. You can attend adult education classes in your local college or special courses that are designed specifically to help businesspeople learn to make effective presentations. And there are many proven techniques in this book, offered by people who are experts in their fields.

Remember, those important skills are just 10 percent of the success that you seek. As you learn and develop the "how to" techniques, be sure to devote some time to the 90 percent, too.

Augment the skills that you are learning, the techniques you are able to develop, with positive attitudes about speaking. Practice what you're learning by experiencing it in your imagination and make it fun! Don't be a spectator, watching yourself speak well. Stay inside of yourself in your imagination. Experience successful performance in your imagination and feel the positive emotions.

And, next time you have an opportunity to stand on your feet and speak to a group, remind yourself that this is one of the joys of your life! Everyone there wants to hear what you're going to say; you know how to express yourself well; and you and the audience are going to have a great time together.

Exciting!

Jim Newman is one of America's pioneers in the study of high-performance behavior and the founder, in 1961, of The PACE Organization. His company conducts PACE seminars and designs special team-building programs for client companies. Jim is author of the best-selling personal development book *Release Your Brakes!* and creator of the PACE PALETTE, a simple, practical tool for identifying individual temperament patterns. When he speaks to company or association meetings, Jim leaves the group with proven tools that have a lasting positive impact on their professional and personal lives.

The Power of Humor 5

Herb True, Ph.D., CPAE
1717 East Colfax
South Bend, IN 46617
219-233-1757
Fax 219-234-2340

Power permeates all our lives. A dozen times a day, we hear or read or speak of power resources, power shortages, power blocks, powers that be, idea power, position power, more power to me. You can be power mad, or you can do a powerful lot of good, depending on whether you have power or power has you. And, there is a special power that can empower you and empower others—it's humor power.

You weren't born with humor power, and you can't buy it. But if you want to be a powerful speaker or presenter, then you need to learn to create and develop your own humor power. Your use of humor power could be a major factor in how your speeches and presentations are accepted and acted upon.

You have probably discovered, as I have, that time after time the thought that people remembered most clearly following a presentation—the idea that an audience member recalls when he or she sees you again, or writes you, or calls you—concerns a message that was wrapped in humor.

Humor has the power to create understanding between strangers. Take an audience that has never seen you before, tell them a funny experience that illustrates how human you are, and they begin to accept you as someone they don't need to feel intimidated by. Share a laugh, and it's probable that you will have established a bond with your audience.

Humor also has the power to change attitudes and perceptions. We've all seen instances where the use of humorous material affects an audience more profoundly than more serious concepts. Audiences seem to be more receptive to a message told on the light, funny side because humor is perceived as a kind, gentle teacher.

Humor isn't scary

It's a common experience to see people nodding in agreement when, in discussing public speaking, one talks about the need to organize one's thoughts or understanding the heterogeneousness of today's audiences. You often get rapt attention when you reinforce your talk with graphs or visual aids. But when you begin talking about using humor, you may see brows wrinkle and faces get serious. That response indicates, to me at least, that the person I am talking with doesn't understand the true nature of humor.

Many think of humor *only* in terms of entertainment, thereby confusing humor with comedy. Comedy is staged laughter, and most often it involves laughing at someone.

When you turn on the television or go to a nightclub, you usually find comedy. In many instances, comedy is banana-peel burlesque aimed directly at making people laugh. Comedians tend to be evaluated by how much laughter they generate. Because much comedic laughter is caused by embarrassment, comedy could be called an artificial form of humor; it often gains success through the degradation of others. I'm not saying comedy is bad; however it may be a questionable source from which an individual can gain the most productive response from a speech or presentation.

Humor, on the other hand, evolves from a creative, right-brained, playful spirit that enables one to treat disappointment with a fond tenderness instead of with antagonism and despair. Humor aims at more than just laughter. It seeks to share merriment, happiness, and joy. Humor is often subtle, relying on an intellectual playfulness while maintaining a basic appeal to the emotions.

Comedy is something that may serve to add to our lives by subtracting from someone else's life, while humor empowers us to add to our lives and to the enjoyment of others by giving the unique gift of ourselves. Humor, rather than laughing at someone else, often involves us laughing at ourselves.

Let me give you an example. My brother is short and heavy. He uses humor effectively by explaining that, when you get on an elevator with him, you better be going down. He also likes to say that it's tough to be short like he is because you can't wear cowboy boots—they cut you under the armpits. I do the same thing with my baldness and the fact that I have eight children.

How humor affects audiences

For the speaker, the major role of humor is often to build a favorable climate. Humor relaxes people and makes them more receptive to one's message. By taking ourselves lightly, we can more readily communicate with others.

Humor serves as a leveling agent; it makes all of us—speaker and audience—equal. Humor helps remove the speaker from the high pedestal, making his or her ideas more appealing to others.

Opening yourself up to others with self-directed humor encourages others to share their feelings, dreams, motives and goals with you. A speaker can actually feel this opening up on the part of his or her audiences, and it's a very rewarding feeling.

Using humor to empower yourself and others isn't reserved

for the precious few. You can learn to employ humor and make your presentation more dramatic and more effective. The key word here is "learn." Humor power doesn't just happen. It takes lots of learning, planning, practice, and work–but it's the kind of work that pays big dividends.

Learning to use humor

While it is true that some people seem more comfortable using humor and therefore use it more naturally, in reality anyone can learn to use humor effectively. Of all the serious humor students I've known, all have become collectors of humor material, whether it is from *Reader's Digest* or Gene Perret's classic *How To Hold Your Audience With Humor.*

Many serious students of humor are subscribers to sources that serve speakers. For example:

- The Executive Speaker. Phone 513-294-8493.
- The American Speaker. Phone 202-337-5980.
- Contemporary Comedy. Phone 214-381-4779.
- Jokes Unlimited. Call Don Wolf, phone 213-876-0830.
- Quote. Call Tom Kelly, phone 505-527-0381.
- Speechwriter Newsletter. Phone 312-335-0037.

While these are all good sources of humor, the truth is that humor is where you find it. Begin looking for things that make you and others you know smile and laugh. Then see how these stories might be used to illustrate your most powerful concepts or truths. When difficult things happen, try to see a funny side to the event or situation, then create a story around what has happened.

Make it a point to tell at least one new story or joke a week to those you talk with. Then practice. Practice will sharpen your delivery and imprint the story in your memory for future use.

Serious students of humor are great at capturing material they have heard other people use. I've seen serious humor students ask others to describe again a humorous situation or tell again a humorous story; the student then repeats the material back to the person to see if he or she has captured the story just right. This kind of attention to detail and polish is important to those who want to become excellent speakers.

Even if a story or joke doesn't work the first time, you will soon learn "savers" such as "That's the first one you've gotten, isn't it, sir?" or, "You better stand up. These are going over your head." Learning some good savers can make you a winner.

Making humor work

Using humor in presentations and speeches doesn't mean that you have to be perceived as a stand-up comic. A spoonful of sincerity and good-naturedness goes a long way toward creating the right atmosphere for your own "think funny" humor.

You may have observed that the real pros personalize every story. They tie in relevant names, locations, and activities to focus their stories and make them more interesting and more appealing.

Professional speakers develop their stories by framing humor with a short, but effective, scenario to establish the situation. Do as they do. Keep it short; speak at a brisk pace; accelerate into a clear punch line. Brevity can be crucial. Nothing kills good material like unnecessary words and detail. Twenty-five to thirty seconds seems for some to be the maximum.

Master the pause; a pause gives your audience time to visualize the material and grasp the situation you are creating so that, when you do deliver the punch line, the effect is much stronger.

Allow yourself to think funny. Don't be afraid to show that you enjoy spreading cheer. Stay focused on your listener's eyes. Capture their attention. Exaggeration can be a big part of humor, so let your face and gestures paint the picture.

Learn the difference between public and private humor. If you must use ethnic, sexual, or religious material, make it at the expense of *your own* ethnic, sexual, or religious group. Here's my rule: If in doubt, leave it out.

Use humor sandwiches. Tell your audience the point you intend to make...then tell the story or joke that illustrates your point. Redundancy helps hammer home your message on all the channels available.

Keep polishing, improving, and using your winners. Don't be afraid to use material many times. Most people like hearing a good performer tell the same story again and again.

Use humor purposefully. All of us have been in an audience when the speaker acted as if he or she was auditioning for a comedy club. Some individuals are so hungry to win the approval of an audience that they will try to find a joke or some kind of material to illustrate every point. That's not the best use of humor. The effective presenter uses humor occasionally, discretely, and deliberately. Have a solid reason for every humorous anecdote or story you share. Try to make sure it gives life to a specific and pertinent point.

When should you use humor?

There is disagreement about whether you should or should not begin a presentation with humorous material. Let's look at both sides.

Many speakers begin with a joke—and that may be a good reason not to do it. You may find it effective to go against what is expected.

In the opening moments of a speech or presentation, it's important to let your audience become accustomed to your voice, the way you look, your mannerisms, etc. So you may not want to waste a valuable piece of material during a period of time when your audience is not yet fully tuned in to you. Save your humor until you've established rapport.

Unless you are perceived by others as a humorist, avoid making humor the major ingredient of your speech. What is the reason you were asked to speak? Probably to inform, to educate, or to inspire—or all of these. Most successful professional presenters aren't really expected to be big-time entertainers. Instead, they use humor to build contrast and to break up heavy material. They use anecdotes to make a point and to lead into the material they most want the audience to remember and act upon.

It's best to avoid repeating jokes or stories you heard only the day or a few days before. Stories and other humorous material run in cycles. So members of your audience are probably hearing the same new material you are.

It's OK to enjoy yourself, but try not to go overboard laughing at your own material. Don't lead the laughter; your audience may feel you are trying to cover up an unfunny story or a comment by responding too prominently yourself.

Avoid stories that are mean-spirited. By this, I mean avoid the kind of humor that shows how you outwitted the other fellow or got the better of the deal. Take a lesson from the great performers who usually use humor to make themselves look foolish, thereby making everyone else feel a little smarter.

Humor "Do's"

Now that I've made some suggestions regarding things to avoid when using humor, let me share with you some things you'll want to do:

• In choosing material, use what you think is funny as a guide. If a particular idea or concept touches your funny bone, it's probable that you can make others smile also when you use it.

• Add authenticity by carrying story material, details, and characteristics into your audience's experience. Adjust a story or an idea by including some comment that you know your audience will identify with.

• Sell your audience on the idea that your material is entertaining. How do you do this? By enjoying the telling, having a sparkle in your eye and an air of suppressed glee about you as you speak. Also, use graphics, props, even magic tricks that you feel will help express the idea visually and graphically.

• Select material that lends itself to telling. Leave out the "he said" and "she said." Impersonate the characters, turning your body to indicate one character speaking to another. Rehearse and rehearse again; practice, practice, practice again before you use material in front of an audience. Master every detail so you will know exactly how and when to use material. This can be enhanced by videotaping or recording your material, then studying it. It's easier if you collect a group of stories, then build them into a vignette. Make them distinctly your own, then use them through the years. You can keep your stories fresh by adjusting details to fit the occasion and the audience.

Discover humor's power

The fact that you are reading this book leads me to believe that you want to become a better speaker and are willing to work toward that goal. If that's true for you, don't overlook the power that humor can bring to every presentation you make.

Most professionals spend hours, days, or years collecting and organizing information for future presentations. Because today's audiences are so visual—they have been trained on Nintendo, MTV, Macintosh icons, and the like—you may find you'll want to add visuals and graphics to enliven your presentations. But don't forget that the thing that empowers every element of every presentation is humor.

Humor power goes deeper than laughter, yields more riches than a smile, delivers more returns than a grin. Humor can ease strain, oil relationships, underline points, reduce tensions, relieve pressures, and generally enhance the quality of one's life. If you can't find some humor in doing whatever you are doing, there is little likelihood that you'll ever do it excellently. Remember this:

Mathematicians can't add without the number two,
Artists can't paint without the color blue,
Authors can't write without the letter "E,"
Musicians can't compose and skip the note of "G."
It's much the same with speaking and every audience you
   meet:
It takes humor power to make a presentation complete.

Herb True holds a Ph.D. in psychology and was co-founder of the Management Development Program at the University of Notre Dame, where he serves as an adjunct professor. His humorous, creative, high-impact, graphic presentations that teach important lessons on management, leadership, and love have earned him the title "The World's Greatest Edu-tainer." In addition to teaching a humor course at the Forever Learning Institute for more than 10 years, Herb has lectured at more than 50 universities in 13 countries. His career as a professional speaker has spanned three decades, and he has addressed over 4,200 groups "from meat packers to chicken pluckers to managers at AT&T and executives at IBM." He is the author of three best-selling humor books and more than 60 booklets and articles appearing in professional journals. He was one of the first recipients of the Council of Peers Award of Excellence (CPAE) presented by members of the National Speakers Association.

Timing Is Everything 6

Don Hutson, CSP, CPAE
The Don Hutson Organization
P.O. Box 172181
Memphis, TN 38187-2181
901-767-0000
800-647-9166
Fax 901-767-5959

You've undoubtedly heard this phrase—*timing is everything*—many times. Timing is everything in investments, in relationship dynamics, in athletics, and in many other things. In making speeches, it is critically important as well.

Audience members are less tolerant than ever of marginal presentation skills, so we should try to give them a good show. One of the single greatest things we can do to enhance the positive impact we have on our listeners is to be keenly aware of timing. If you master the principles of good timing, you will be more of a pleasure to listen to, and your audience will retain more. You will be a far better speaker by mastering this one skill.

Today, people's time is more valuable than ever. If you are to give a 40-minute talk to 150 people, you are charged with being skilled enough and informative enough to justify 100 "man hours" being invested in hearing you. Be good so that you can have pride in the fact that you touched those people in a positive way!

I get anywhere from two to 12 calls a month from people who want to take me to lunch to discuss getting into the speaking business. When I was president of the National Speakers Association in 1977, we had about 275 to 300 members. At the time of this writing, NSA has almost 4,000 members. There's a speaker under every rock! I mention this to impress people with how competitive this profession is today and how tough it is to really impress listeners.

Brian Tracy and I were recently discussing what to tell people who are thinking about the world of professional speaking. Brian asks them, "What do you have the ability to tell people in a truly effective manner that they don't already know?" This is a penetrating and challenging question. People who have trouble answering this question are premature in their vision of being a skilled speaker, whether amateur or professional.

On the other hand, just as you have heard that everyone has a book in them, maybe everyone also has a speech in them. Just don't take the opportunity or the responsibility lightly.

In our quest for presentation excellence, it is important to understand that timing can be the difference between a good speech and a great speech—and with little or no variance in subject matter. What kind of timing is important? There are several elements of a speech in which timing is critical.

The butterflies syndrome

The less comfortable you are, the poorer your timing will be. I'm convinced that the best way to fight nervousness—to "get your butterflies to fly in formation"—and to get your timing down is to be so well prepared that you know little, if anything, is going to go wrong. This will give you confidence and direction and will enable you to concentrate on good timing.

One way to enhance confidence and timing is to construct your presentation with the "vignette system." Most professionals do this, and it is the best way I know of to prepare a well-timed speech. A vignette is simply a stand-alone story. Practice a vignette until you have the timing down and know exactly how long it takes you to tell it. Tie it into your subject matter with an appropriate segue such as "To illustrate this point, let me tell you about an experience I had when I was a sophomore in college...", followed by what you know is a six-minute story or vignette.

Speaking icon Bill Gove says that most people make speech-making harder than it is. He suggests simple guidelines such as "Don't ever make a speech longer than 20 minutes unless you are being paid." (Most professional speakers agree that the longer the speech, the easier it is to make!) Develop several good vignettes and decide before a speech which ones best fit the group you are addressing and in what sequence—and then do it! When you know how long each vignette is, you can design your speech accordingly. If you can comfortably deliver each vignette, you will comfortably deliver your speech. This is the big picture of timing.

"Uh...you know"

"Uh" and "You know" are the best examples available of what is known as *pause-fillers*. Pause-fillers do more than any other single thing to destroy what could be excellent timing.

Develop the habit of not using these or other pause-fillers. The best way to keep from committing this oratorical sin is to record every talk you give so that you can listen to it and study your timing, including the use of pause-fillers. This will also give you the opportunity to study the value and impact of every component of your speech, enabling you to rationally expand, contrast, or eliminate stories in order to improve your speech.

What's going on? Give me a clue!

One component of timing and speech effectiveness is *what* you say and *when* you say it. Is your subject matter in logical sequence? Does it flow and make sense to the listener in that sequence? Listening to you should be an enjoyable experience, not hard labor.

Dale Carnegie used to teach the "Tell, tell, tell" technique of speaking. Tell them what you're going to tell them. Tell them. Then, tell them what you told them. This makes sense. Err on the side of simplicity, not complexity, in speech organization.

I am asked to emcee numerous charitable events in my home base of Memphis, and I do them when I'm in town. Frankly, I get lots of compliments each time, and I'm going to give you my secret formula now!

Step One: Start exactly on time. Most people running meetings just can't start on time. I think many people are putting it off because they are scared to approach the microphone. Don't look for a reason not to start. Starting on time is really very simple—Just do it! If there are a few people still in the corridors, they'll normally come in when you convene the meeting.

Step Two: Keep the program rolling and make sure everything happens on time. You should clarify time allotments in advance with everyone on your agenda.

Step Three: Conclude the program on time and adjourn the meeting.

No bells—no whistles—no oratorical heights of excellence. Just be on time.

Go with the flow

What do you do if the person running the meeting wants you to expand or cut your talk by 10 minutes?

Rule #1: Do it!

Rule #2: If you are tempted not to comply, see Rule #1.

I think it is important for us to respond to the meeting planner's need, so be prepared to handle the unexpected. If you are uptight about expanding your talk, just devote extra time to fielding questions.

Is he at the right meeting?

The single most powerful means of assuring speech-making success is to tailor your remarks to your audience.

Be a good information gatherer. Ask lots of questions of more than one person prior to your appearance. If audience members know you've done your homework, they will appreciate you more and respond better. The more time and energy you devote to tailoring, the more impressed your audience will be.

A well-known sports figure recently opened his speech with this line: "I don't have any idea what you folks do, but I guess it doesn't matter since I'm just going to tell you a little about my baseball career." This is an insult to everyone in the audience.

What's the bottom line?

How long is the opening of your speech? If your introductory remarks go on for too long, your audience will get impatient and your timing will be off at a critically important juncture in your presentation.

Incidentally, I have a pet peeve I would like to suggest that you avoid in getting your talk started. I've heard speakers say, "Before I start my program, I want to tell you something of special importance about..." Hey, you've already started! The moment you take over the microphone, your performance has begun. Don't try to separate your prepared remarks from something that comes across as an announcement. Weave every component of your presentation together masterfully so that it flows well, and you will demonstrate much better timing.

The pause that refreshes

One of the greatest techniques of speech-making is the pause. Learn everything you can about the power of the pause. I have always had a rather rapid-fire delivery. For years, I used the pause poorly. I simply had not thoroughly learned the skill.

A few years ago at our Speakers Roundtable meeting, we hired Ron Arden, a professional acting coach with decades of experience in London theatre, to critique us. (See Ron's epilogue at the end of this book.) Each of us gave a vignette of about 10 to 20 minutes, after which Ron unloaded on us. After my fast-paced delivery of some of my material on leadership style, I sat down. Ron Arden paused (the audience needed it!) and said, "I'm exhausted!"

His remarks were among the greatest lessons I have ever learned about timing and the power of the pause. Here's a simple synopsis:

1. Pauses are good, not bad.
2. Pauses give an audience time to consider and digest what they hear.
3. Pauses help the speaker better articulate the material.
4. Silence is a powerful attention-getter.
5. Pauses improve the emphasis of your variability of tone and inflection.

Watch where you step

Have you ever heard the phrase "He stepped on my line"? Its general connotation implies that one person started talking while the other person was still talking. It's a bad habit and rude behavior.

I know some speakers who have a similar habit: They step on *their own lines* or audience responses! This can destroy timing. Be sure you finish one sentence or thought before beginning another. Also, when you get positive audience response like a good laugh or applause, don't step on it. Let it reach its normal conclusion, then resume speaking. Milk the positives for all they are worth.

And now, our late speaker...

Surely 98 percent of the time you get on late will be because the meeting is running late, at no fault of yours. If the program is running late, don't forget to ask the coordinator of the event before going on, "Charles, I was scheduled from 8:00 until 9:00, and it's 8:20 now. Do you want me to give the full one-hour presentation, or cut it to 40 minutes to keep you on schedule?" This is a very important timing issue. If you are being paid, keep the customer happy and respond to his wishes. If you are not getting paid, it's still his meeting, right?

By the way, if you are ever late for a meeting where you are to speak, it is going to be a high stress event for you. Always give yourself plenty of time by arriving well before your announced starting time.

Sudden death overtime

This is not just a phrase for athletics; it applies to your speech as well! Don't commit oratorical suicide by going over your allotted time. There are many wonderful reasons to end your presentation on time. Here are some:

1. People will often respond to a good talk that ends on time by saying, "Wow, is it over already? The time flew by." This is an excellent compliment to the speaker.

2. You leave them hungry for more which precipitates remarks like "I could have listened another hour to that speaker!" Better to leave them hungry than overfed and staring at their watches. It can also precipitate additional future invitations (if that is one of your goals).

3. It is professional and respectful of your audience's time to end on time.

4. You do your fair share to keep the overall agenda intact and on time. When you go overtime, you are fair game to the critiquers.

5. There are some people who have other commitments and will get up and leave during your talk if you go overtime. This disrupts audience concentration and can hamper your continuity at a critical moment.

A significant percentage of speeches given would have been better received if they had ended sooner. This is one of the toughest lessons a speechmaker must learn. Some professionals are even bad about this (a shame!). I guess some people get addicted to positive response and crave just a little more of it when a speech is going well. This is unprofessional and uncalled for. Watch out for this temptation because it isn't fair to whoever or whatever program follows. You steal their time and cause an audience anguish.

I wish I had a nickel for every time I have heard a fellow audience member say, "This would have been a great speech if the speaker had stopped 15 minutes ago." Or, "What's the deal? Can't this clown tell time?" One of my mentors (who shall remain nameless here) was one of the greatest speakers who ever lived, but he had this problem. He was so intelligent that I could not believe he never figured this out.

Some of the best training for getting your point across succinctly and effectively with no waste of time is Toastmasters. I know of no one who can't learn from this beneficial organization. Toastmasters emphasizes this principle: End on time.

I could sure use a laugh

Humor is one of the most powerful contributors to speaking talent, along with good timing. This does not necessarily mean joke-telling either. The best humor is usually a one-liner tailored to a current situation. Work diligently on good, quality one-liners, and intersperse them throughout your talk at logical intervals. This will contribute greatly to your timing. Always try to make your humor pertinent and illustrative of a point. Here are some examples of one-liners I use:

• Some people say motivation doesn't last. A bath doesn't either—but it's a good idea to take one once in a while.

• I asked the boss how many people he had working for him, and he said about half of 'em!

It may not seem fair, but our audience members are well-entertained people seeing the world's best speakers, comedians, and entertainers daily on TV—and that's who we, as speakers, are being compared to. Appropriate use of humor makes the talk seem shorter, and it's considerably more enjoyable to experience. Humor is an excellent tool for improving timing.

"I gotta question"

Is there to be a question-and-answer period following your speech? Clear understanding of the game plan by all parties is imperative. Is the time you have been allotted to include a Q&A period? Does the person running the meeting want you to speak for the announced time frame you have been given and expect you to field questions beyond that amount of time? Has this been discussed? Always do so, since we can't treat time casually! Remember, five minutes is really 500 minutes if you have 100 people in the audience.

How are you in a Q&A session? How does that (very different) skill compare with your speaking skill? You may want to announce that your 30 minutes will be 20 minutes of remarks, followed by 10 minutes of Q&A.

I addressed an insurance company convention recently in Cancun along with Joe Gibbs, the former coach of the Washington Redskins. Joe is a pretty good speaker, but his skill in handling questions and thinking fast of creative, interesting answers is extraordinary. This is a case where, in my opinion, he would be better off devoting more time to Q&A and less to formal remarks. Even a less-than-good speaker can be well received if the Q&A session goes extremely well. Think timing.

"In conclusion..."

Don't ever say "In conclusion" unless you are within two

minutes of relinquishing the lectern. There have been many listeners made weary by speakers who tested them with the "In conclusion..." line, only to punish them for 15 to 20 additional minutes.

Lombardi was right

In conclusion (I promise!), remember the words of the great Vincent Lombardi who said, "Nobody ever attained greatness in anything who was not willing to continuously practice, drill, and rehearse."

Practice your timing, and you *will* be a better speaker. Good luck!

Don Hutson's career in speaking, management, and sales have brought him many honors. He worked his way through the University of Memphis, graduating at age 20 with a major in sales. A 28-year veteran of the professional speaking and training business, Don has given over 4,500 speeches and seminars, and he has addressed over 300 of the Fortune 500 companies. He speaks on "High Performance Selling," "Leadership Makes the Difference," and "How to Make and Keep Customers Happy." He is past president of the National Speakers Association and recipient of both the Cavett Award and the International Speakers Hall of Fame Award. Don is also the author of *The Sale* and is the co-author of *Insights into Excellence.*

Speak From Your Strengths

7

Daniel Burrus, CSP, CPAE
Burrus Research Associates, Inc.
P.O. Box 26413
Milwaukee, WI 53226-0413
414-786-2308
800-827-6770
Fax 414-786-3022

During the past 12 years, I have delivered over 1,200 keynote speeches to audiences ranging in size from 50 people to 6,000 and on four continents. Because of my experience, people often ask me what it takes to give a successful speech, which I define as a powerful presentation that conveys a lasting message. In this chapter, I will attempt to answer that question by sharing with you some information and ideas I have gathered, tested, and evaluated while learning to be an effective speaker myself. Whether you are new to speaking or are a seasoned veteran, I believe these ideas can and will work for you.

One of the real keys to becoming a good speaker is to learn your own unique strengths and weaknesses, then focus on maximizing your strengths. On the following pages, I will help you learn to look for your strengths as you assess each speaking opportunity that comes your way.

Start with the basics

What kind of speaking are you good at now, or could you learn to do well? To answer this question, let's examine the territory.

Most speakers are usually classified as being one of the following: informational, humorous/entertaining, or motivational. In addition, there are three basic types of presentations, and they are easiest to define by their length and the degree of audience participation:

• A **speech** is a presentation that can be as long as 90 minutes with little or no direct audience participation.

• A **seminar** is a half- or full-day presentation and often involves some audience participation.

• A **workshop** is a multi-day training session that involves a high degree of audience participation and a small amount of actual presentation time.

Are you at your best giving short speeches, half-day presentations, full-day seminars, or multiple-day training sessions? If your answer is, "I'm great at all of these," you didn't answer the question. Which are you *best* at?

There are very few professional speakers—if any—who are great at all three types of presentations. Presentations of differing lengths demand different "natural" skills. Training techniques used in a workshop are very different from the more interactive speaking techniques used in a seminar, or the more focused speaking techniques used in a speech.

What are your natural skills? Do they lend themselves to high-energy speeches, or to longer sessions in which you have more time to express your ideas? Are you a good motivator but not such a good teacher—or just the opposite? If you have found that you are best in a half-day or longer situation, then that is the type of presentation length you should accept most often. You have found your optimum presenting niche.

Ninety percent of my presentations are a special type of speech called a keynote speech. When I first started speaking, I knew a general definition of the term keynote speech, but I was short on specific knowledge. Before you agree to deliver one, you need to know more!

A keynote speaker delivers a major speech at a meeting or convention; a number of other speakers are usually making presentations at the same meeting or convention. Frequently, a professional speaker will be used for the keynote, but not always. Sometimes a famous person or well-known industry expert will deliver the keynote address. Everyone at the meeting attends the keynote speech; most of the other presentations are either break-out sessions running concurrently or, at smaller meetings, the presenters may be in-house people such as the company president, the head of marketing, or a tax specialist.

What really separates a keynote speech from the rest is its purpose. The keynote might be the opening presentation with the purpose being to set the tone and theme of the convention. It might be the closing speech with the purpose being to tie all of the events together and let the audience go home feeling inspired, positive, and glad they attended. The keynote might be delivered in the morning, in the evening, or at lunch. There may even be several keynote speakers at the same convention, usually one keynote speaker per day.

The demands for giving a keynote are different from other types of speeches. It will take more time to prepare for a keynote than a non-keynote speech. Unlike the other speakers, the keynote speaker needs to know about the overall objectives of the entire convention as well as the needs of everyone in attendance. What is important is that you understand what will be expected of you if you agree to deliver a keynote address or if you agree to conduct a seminar, lead a workshop, or deliver another type of speech.

What is your speaking energy level?

When I finish a keynote speech, my shirt tends to be wet with sweat. This isn't because I jump and run around; it's because of the focused power I put into the message. I feel as though I have taken all of the energy it takes to deliver an eight-hour seminar and used it in that keynote. I have found that the more of a work-out I feel I have been through, the better the keynote. If you like that type of feeling, if you think you are best in that time frame, keynotes are something you should try to develop.

Within each speaker lies an optimum length presentation. If you are new to speaking, experiment and find out what suits you best. If you are a seasoned pro, ask yourself if you are capitaliz-ing on doing what you are best at, accepting opportunities that allow you to utilize your strengths and thus advance your reputa-tion and your career, or are you delivering whatever a meeting planner currently needs?

Find your focus

Ask yourself, "What is my purpose in delivering this speech? Who do I want to benefit from my words and ideas?"

If you are focused on giving a speech that sounds well-pre-pared and allows you to show off your talent as a speaker, it will fall far short of what it could have been. When your focus is on helping the audience rather than on glorifying yourself, you will have the ability to touch lives and truly make a difference. Only when you show you care will the minds and hearts of the audi-ence be receptive to your words. The topic of the speech is not as important as the focus of the speaker. Focus on the audience and their needs!

Have topic credibility

Ask yourself, "Do I have the credibility to speak on this topic?" If your answer is no, don't give the speech! It is imper-ative that the audience perceives that you have earned the right to address them on your topic. Your introduction should establish that credibility.

Always write your own introduction. It should take no longer than one minute to read. The main focus of your introduction should be to answer this question: What gives me the right to speak on this topic?

Treat your topic in a unique way

Ask yourself, "Do I have a unique approach to this topic?" Today's audiences are far more sophisticated than in years past; they attend many meetings and probably belong to one or more professional organizations. It is safe to assume that they have heard someone speak on your topic before.

The best way to give your topic a unique approach is to share personal stories and situations relevant to the topic. This is an opportunity for you to speak from your strengths, sharing with your audience insights and experiences that only you can share.

Paint verbal portraits

Remember the old saying, "A picture is worth a thousand words"? Help your audiences see a picture in their minds as you speak. Let me give you an example.

I was in an airport recently, and there was a gate agent standing at the gate. A small child was standing near the entrance. The gate agent looked down at the child and said, "Don't go down the ramp!" Guess where the kid went? You're right! Just a few minutes after the gate agent finished his sentence, the kid went down the ramp.

Why do kids always seem to do what you tell them not to do? It's because they think in terms of pictures. "Don't" isn't a picture, so what do they really hear? "Go down the ramp!"

If you say to a child, "Don't wet your bed tonight," guess what will happen? But if you say, "Leave your bed dry tonight," you'll have a better chance of communicating your meaning. Remember, adults are just grown-up kids. We process information best when it is in picture form.

Care about your subject

Do you have a burning passion for your topic? The level of passion you feel for your topic is the most critical element of a keynote speech as well as most other types of presentations. Without passion, the speech will tend to drag. Passion for your topic is so powerful, it can even make up for a weak presentation style.

Many speakers start out with a joke to break the ice. A joke by itself usually isn't strong enough, particularly if you are not a great humorist. Instead, you could have your opening statement tell your audience that you know something they don't know—but they *need* to know. Your ending should link to this opening statement with a very strong, upbeat call for action. When you truly believe you are helping your audience to learn and grow, you will find fire to ignite your speeches. Don't accept a speaking assignment unless you feel the potential for this kind of fire.

Speak from your heart

Reading a speech is the least effective way to convey a message; it is too impersonal. The best method is to speak without any notes. If this is not possible, hide your notes in your visuals.

I always use visuals. Studies show that people remember 10 percent of what they read, 20 percent of what they hear, 30 percent of what they see, and 50 percent of what they see and hear. In addition, studies on retention show that audiences retain 10 percent of the information when only a lecture style is used, 50 percent when visuals are added, 70 percent when audience involvement is added, and 83 percent when involvement and visuals are combined.

Visuals communicate ideas faster than the spoken word alone; visuals tend to arouse and hold the interest of the audience; visuals help to explain complicated ideas more easily. Here are some tips I have collected through the years regarding working with visuals:

• Keep the room light high to keep the energy levels high. The audience needs to see the speaker, the speaker should be able to see at least some of the audience, and the audience should be able to see their notes, if they choose to write any, as well as the visuals. If one has to suffer, it should be the visuals, not the audience or the speaker.

• Overheads are good for seminars or training sessions, but not keynotes.

• I always use slides in my presentations. Computer-projected information will work in small groups (up to 75), but the room light has to be too low, and the definition of the words and graphics are too coarse for larger groups at this time.

In the next few years, video projection systems will advance so that they will be bright and sharp enough for large group presentations without having to turn the lights way down. At that time, you might want to try using a CD-I system (compact disk interactive) or Video-CD.

Be yourself

I have seen many speakers step on stage and become someone else. You can't fool an audience. It is important to appear genuine on stage, and the only way to do that is to be yourself. By maximizing your authenticity, you will leverage your personal uniqueness into a powerful tool for empowering audiences to take positive actions.

Become one with your audience

Is this an audience you understand, would like to know better, feel comfortable with? Are you willing to expend the time and energy it will take to prepare a message that is meaningful for those who will hear it?

Getting to know your audience is essential if you want to make a difference in their lives. It is not enough to have a good speech. You need to know as much about the group as possible to frame your key concepts in a way that will make them relevant to the audience's world.

I always ask the meeting planner to fill out a pre-program questionnaire. What are this audience's shared concerns? Problems? Issues and triumphs? The night before I will speak, I try to put myself in their shoes, become one with their wants and needs. By the time I begin my speech, I will be thinking as one of them.

Once I was asked to give an after-dinner speech to a management group. After talking with a few people before dinner began, I asked the meeting planner if there was anything new that had happened to the company or the audience since our last communication. I was told that they had all been laid off at the end of the day and had decided to go to tonight's meeting in order to say good-bye. No one, including the meeting planner, told me this important information until I asked the question!

Use the power of focus

Remember when you were a child and held a magnifying glass between the sun and a piece of paper? The sunlight was focused in a single direction, and the paper started to burn. Focus is power!

People who are asked to deliver speeches tend to be idea people. The problem with being an idea person is that you always have another one. This causes you to lose your focus.

You could speak on a variety of topics. You may even have credentials and experience for each one. But as you increase the number of topics you speak on, you decrease the power of focus. In addition, the more topics you offer a meeting planner, the harder their decision becomes. Ask yourself, "How focused is my subject?" Keep in mind that it is very difficult to become a known authority on several topics.

Be adaptive

There's truth in the old saying, "What can go wrong *will* go wrong." The key is to solve problems before they happen.

Always check the room in which you will be speaking at least

45 minutes before the meeting starts. If you wait until the break just before you speak, there may not be time to maximize the environment for your best presentation. Checking the room early will give you time to test the microphones, lights, staging, and visuals and make any needed changes without having to rush and lose your focus.

Over the years, I have had to adapt to many unanticipated situations. Some examples include:

• A major power outage occurring as I began my presentation,

• Wireless microphones going out in the middle of my speech,

• A pitcher of ice water spilling on the lap of someone in the audience as I started speaking,

This could be a very long list...

When something happens—and it will—don't try to ignore it. The audience's attention will go to the event and stay there. Instead, use the event to your advantage by acknowledging the situation in a humorous way. This will let you quickly regain control of the situation and bring your audience back to what you are saying.

When asked to speak, regardless of the format, you are provided with an opportunity to make a difference in many people's lives. Non-professional speakers tend to spend too much time focusing on their speaking weaknesses. Instead, focus on your natural speaking strengths. A "natural" speaking style that allows you to be yourself on stage will always give you the ability to be the best that you can be.

D aniel Burrus, CSP, CPAE, one of the world's leading technology forecasters, is the founder and president of Burrus Research Associates, Inc., a research and consulting firm that specializes in global innovations in technology, their creative application, and their future impact. Over the past 12 years, he has established a near-perfect record of accurately predicting the future of technological change. He is the author of six books that have been published since 1990. His best selling book, *Technotrends*, has been translated into over a dozen languages and is available on four continents. He has delivered over 1,200 speeches worldwide.

What I Teach Some of America's Most Successful Executives

8

Ty Boyd, CSP, CPAE
Ty Boyd Enterprises, Inc.
The Cullen Center
1727 Garden Terrace
Charlotte, NC 28203
704-333-9999
800-336-2693
Fax 704-333-0207

I've been asked many times, "What are the most important and essential ingredients to making a successful presentation?" The answer to this question is very important, for the correct answer to the question is also a key to unlocking the door of success. In exploring the answer, we'll be discussing the most important leadership skill, the most important selling skill, in truth, one of the greatest *success* skills there is.

For about 25 years now, I have been a professional presenter. I've presented programs on five continents, and my audiences have included over a million people. For better than 13 of those 25 years, I've conducted a two-and-one-half day presentations skills course called the Excellence in Speaking Institute (ESI). Participants have come from every walk of life, every station and experience level—men and women, from every state in the union, every province of Canada, and several foreign countries.

They are young, old, experienced, inexperienced, successful, and unproven. And what we've learned is this: *Almost without exception, those who decide to really work on their presentation skills can become dramatically more effective!*

Those who participate in the ESI course learn to harness their enthusiasm to the skills they can develop or currently have. They focus like a laser, and they become very successful. If you are willing to stretch, to grow, to risk some short-term discomfort in employing heretofore undeveloped speaking tools, you too can heighten the impact of your presentations.

To set the record straight, let me declare that speaking skills are a critically important component of leadership and selling. I believe an even more important success skill is the ability to listen. In my view, it is much tougher to learn to be a really good listener than it is to improve your presentation skills. So here's my first advice to you if you want to become a better presenter: *Work on your listening skills.* Listening well will help you to gain communications mastery.

How we learn

Now back to presentation mastery. We learn by internalizing information and by actively using it. This requires risking, challenging our own comfort level, and trusting the source. It also means not giving up, doing something again and again.

It has been said that the number one fear of professionals in America is the fear of speaking, of presenting. This causes the non-professional speaker sometimes to approach speaking with a "not to lose" attitude rather than playing to win. So, I want you to read this chapter with an open mind. You won't be able to employ all the ideas at once. That would be impossible. Try a new twist or two each time you present.

If your new practices don't work perfectly for you at first, don't be discouraged. Don't stop. Keep on. I've been at this for 25 years, and I continue to learn new uses of the tools of presenting. Just be aware that you have a whole tool chest filled with wonderfully expressive instruments. Don't fear using them.

You probably won't use those instruments like a pro at first. You can't expect to be a major leaguer your first time at bat, but keep on. You can become a superlative presenter if you are willing to practice. That's the way every great athlete reaches his or her potential. Speaking requires the same pursuit. It's called mastery.

Now, Ty's Ten Top Tips on building a powerful presentation.

Ty's Tip One: Have "fire in your belly"

The most important ingredient in successful communication is energy. Speak with conviction. Choose topics about which you are passionate. If you will have fire in your belly for your subject, success is almost guaranteed.

That fire can be expressed in many ways. Some speakers have highly-charged styles, but some of the most energetic people I have ever met seldom speak above a whisper. You can see the energy in their eyes, in their body movement. You can feel it in the impact of their words. You can sense that fire in their total presentation.

Ty's Tip Two: Have focus

Don't ramble. Build your presentation around three or four well-defined points. Support those main points with both facts and feelings. The first tells, the latter sells! Learn to use a tight outline and lean verbiage. This makes for clear understanding.

Don't ramble around the platform while you are presenting. By rambling, I mean purposeless wandering. Many people ill-advisedly walk, wander, and pace as they speak. What they are attempting to do is to dissipate their own extra energy. This dilutes the focus of the messenger and wears out the audience at the same time.

Here's a better way: Center yourself. Stand with your weight equally distributed on two feet. Speak directly to the audience.

Stand tall. Make your point. You certainly are encouraged to walk if there is a reason to move. We are not looking for a statue—but, on the other hand, neither are we looking for a rolling river. So focus on your content and on its presentation with laser-like aim.

In opening, you'll want to capture the audience's attention with a "grabber opener" such as a startling fact, a powerful question, a joke, a quote, etc. Speak in specifics, but many successful speakers learn to do so as a storyteller. I'm often asked why so many preachers, teachers, authors, and speakers come from the South. My answer is that I believe it's the result of the South's storyteller culture. The message must be clearly outlined and thought out, but it's the messenger's presentation skills that make it powerful.

Dr. Albert Morabian's research tells us that seven percent of our message is the verbiage we use, 38 percent the way we use those words, and 55 percent is the unspoken elements of the communication. So, the words are critically important, but it's clearly the presentation mastery of the messenger that makes a speech effective.

A word or two about practice. A secret of the great presenters is first in knowing the material, then concentrated practice of its delivery. Too often, you and I have had experience in "winging it"—just making a presentation off the tops of our heads. We may think, "Boy, this is the way to do it. I am at my best when I 'wing it'." Hold on!

Let me ask you a question. Would you bet on a performer who only winged his or her performance—a golfer, a baseball player, or a singer? A tennis player, a salesperson, or a leader? No. I don't know any great presenters who don't also rehearse and practice. The great George Burns is reported to have said, "I did essentially the same act on stage for 23 years." Twenty-three years! "But," George Burns continued, "I never once did my act on stage without first having practiced it in my room." So, the clear message to you is not to "wing it." Focus your presentation. Then practice, practice, practice.

Ty's Tip Three: Good speakers perform

You are performing at this very moment as you read this chapter. I am performing at this very moment as I write. There is a clear difference between acting and performing. *Acting* is when you play the part of someone else, say, Julius Caesar or Madame Curie. You use your own skills to portray that person. *Performing* is using those same tools to play yourself. We have deep tool boxes. And because we're always performing, I suggest that we should perform at our best. Make that performance powerful. Put your whole self into the presentation. If the performance suffers, the content is of little value.

Use illustrations. The listener is hungry for pictures. Use color. Don't be bland, black and white. Use color! *Be exciting!* You'll want to be sure you limit the use of pictures and slides to a supporting role, however. Don't become just a voice for a group of colorful pictures and other visuals. There is an art to using computer graphics, slides, flip charts, and support documents. Make them support your performance. Always practice with them before you actually speak. Their skillful use will enhance your performance.

Ty's Tip Four: Use color

Voice color. *Body* color. *Energy* color. Use vocal variety in order to avoid a black and white, bland, monotonous presentation.

We must fight many forms of monotony. Present with high energy only, and our presentations become monotonous. If we use low energy all the time that, too, becomes monotonous. If we pause at predictable times, we become monotonous. Obviously, what we do *not* want is monotony. We want the antithesis of monotony, which is a colorful presentation. Create vocal variety! Learn to whisper and to shout. Speed up and slow down. Pause, pause some more. Get high notes and low notes. Use your entire vocal scale.

In broadcast (which is where I started at age 15), I learned that the broadcast medium itself will somehow eliminate about 30 percent of your voice color. So, broadcasters are taught to be nearly excessive in their vocal color. By the time it's heard, it is less colorful. Well, the speaking platform can do the same. The telephone, too! So, learn to use more color than you have used before.

Use your entire vocal scale. Think of your voice as a fine violin, or an oboe, or a clarinet. It doesn't have to be deep and bass-like or sultry and sexy to be great. It can be a beautiful violin or flute. You can create tones that are alive and colorful. You'll have to work on that. A practice point: Read from a newspaper or magazine out loud 10 or 15 minutes at a time, several times a week. Stretch your vocal scale. This will help you to increase the color of your voice.

By the way, your friends will probably not notice that you are changing the color of your voice, but they will discover you have become more effective. You may even feel very phony and uncomfortable using more vocal color on your first try, but trust me. Do it. Add color.

Ty's Tip Five: Learn to use your eyes

Our eyes are our second most powerful tool of communication. If your belly's on fire for your subject, your eyes will tell the story.

Let me put you in a strange land. You don't know the language. They don't know yours. You know how to articulate the story powerfully, but if they can't understand your words, your message is lost unless your eyes and body tell the story. Make no mistake about this: Eye-to-eye contact with your audience is powerful! The eyes really are "the windows of the soul."

As you speak, make eye contact with one person, then finish your sentence or thought. Let your eyes linger. Then, look at another person. Make your contact one to three seconds. Talk to one person at a time. This is so much more effective than sweeping the masses casually or looking over their heads. This practice alone will make you far more personal, more intimate, and more effective as a presenter. You will connect.

Here's another tip: If you look at a large audience collectively, that sea of faces can really frighten you. But, if you will look at those faces one at a time, you will see them as just plain people who are interested in you and want to connect with you.

Ty's Tip Six: Use your face

The greatest bank account we have in human relations is absolutely free. It's a smile. Add your smile to penetrating eyes and expressive brows. With your eyes on fire, and an intensely interesting face, you'll capture the attention of even the most calloused person.

Your face is really like a television set. People are accustomed to watching a lot of action on that television screen. People will watch your face with more interest if there is color and energy in the picture. People will watch a television longer than they'll watch a radio! Your face can create entertaining excitement that enhances your presentation.

Ty's Tip Seven: Use the rest of your body parts, too!

After your eyes and face comes the other important carrier of the message: your body. Add the power of your body by standing tall, by using gestures.

As a practice point in our Excellence in Speaking Institute, we suggest that when rehearsing, the participants overemphasize key areas: overemphasize gestures, overemphasize pauses, overemphasize energy, overemphasize facial expressions, etc. We explain that you won't make your actual presentation with that much boldness, but you will have expanded your comfort zone and will actually be using more of your tools. Make bold rather than timid gestures and broad as well as subtle movement.

Great stage performers have learned their bodies, faces, and eyes are essential to telling the whole story most effectively.

Ty's Tip Eight: Maintain physical balance

Earlier we talked about centering your power. A great part of centering is related to balance. There's a subtle difference in the respect awarded those who stand tall with their weight equally balanced on both feet. You lose none of your warmth and appeal by standing tall. You gain stature and a sense of power.

Earlier I said it's OK to walk, but to do so with a purpose. Don't wander aimlessly, pacing and creating a cadence of movement. This becomes monotonous. It wears down your audience, rendering you far less effective. The audience will not award you as much respect and trust if you wander. Stand still. Don't pace. Move when there is a purpose in doing so. Stand tall. Speak with authority.

Ty's Tip Nine: Involve your audience

Be sensitive to the audience's needs. If there are 10 people in your audience, there are 10 different sets of needs.

If possible, get to know your audience before you speak. I do everything I can to arrive early in order to meet members of the audience. I learn their individual interests and weave them into my presentation. This makes the message so much more personal. And it also provides a measure of comfort for the presenter as well! Remember, balance your emphasis on both content and relationships, facts *and feelings*.

You must strive to answer the multiple needs of an audience. You cannot be all things to all people, but you can create a balance of information, entertainment, and involvement for your audience.

Ty's Tip Ten (and the most important rule of all): Practice, practice, practice!

Never take a speaking engagement lightly. If you are to do

your best, you must practice and practice and practice. It's not only what you say, but how you say it. "Winging it" is a very common trap, one that many presenters fall into. They say, "I am best when I don't practice." The danger of this is *sometimes* a winger does do a great job. So she may then assume that she is most effective without practice. You must not let this mistake happen to you. It's a guarantee of failure or at the most, mediocrity.

Ask Michael Jordan how many hours he practiced for every minute on the court. Ask golfer Jack Nicklaus. Ask Mia Hamm, the great UNC All American soccer star. Ask a star salesperson. Ask Barbara Jordan, Billy Graham, Lee Iacocca, Patricia Fripp, Zig Ziglar, Naomi Rhode. The greats practice. No exceptions!

Sometimes our greatest presentations or our greatest opportunities to close the sale are done in a question-and-answer period. Conclusion: When a question-and-answer period is appropriate, rehearse answering key questions just as diligently as you rehearse your talk. This is particularly true if there is the possibility of controversy or really tough questions.

Politicians know this. Industry leaders know it. Identify the four or five toughest questions that might be asked. Then prepare a rehearsed answer for each of those. Don't wait to practice on your audience. Practice long before the actual performance.

And finally, a couple of odds and ends:

• Stimulants do not make you sharper. They are, at best, treacherous friends. No alcohol before speaking, ever.

• Off-color material and four-letter words are hardly ever necessary. They will offend someone in every audience. Don't resort to cheap laughs, uneasy applause. The price is too great.

Well, there you have it, quick and simple. Ten powerful tips on how to make a powerful presentation to any size group, from two to two thousand. The skills are essentially the same, only the dynamics change with the size of the audience and the setting.

Now, all that remains for *you* to do is to use these tools in your next presentation. Adjust. Try them again. Have trusted advisors view your efforts. Listen to their feedback. Practice. Practice. Practice.

To gain additional skills, consider joining a Toastmasters organization. Look for source books on making presentations and speeches in your library or your bookstore. Decide that you are going to double your effectiveness by fine-tuning your own presentation skills.

Learning to be a better presenter and a better speaker is a *money skill*. You will be personally rewarded for your efforts. There are few satisfactions that equal the feeling of having made an exciting and effective presentation. I wish you many! *You can!* Do it!

Ty Boyd, CSP, CPAE, is a businessman, broadcaster, author, and professional speaker. For 25 years, he has enjoyed top billing during one of corporate America's most exciting eras. Entertaining, vital keynotes complement the extended training his company offers in communications, leadership, and customer-focused service. In 1982, Ty founded the Excellence in Speaking Institute (ESI), which features an intensive, limited-enrollment, video-feedback presentations skills course. ESI graduates represent every state and province in North America. Courses are conducted in Charlotte, North Carolina, as open seminars, as well as on-site for corporate clients. In 1995, Ty expanded his training company with the formation of The Academy of Emerging Leaders. The Academy provides vital communication skills for young, fast-trackers in a variety of professions.

Preparing For Your Speech

9

Tony Alessandra, Ph.D., CSP, CPAE
Alessandra & Associates
P.O. Box 2767
La Jolla, CA 92038-2767
619-459-4515
800-222-4383
Fax 619-459-0435

Once you have accepted a speaking engagement, it is imperative that you do all you can to prepare for it. All things being equal, the better your preparation, the more successful your speech is likely to be.

There are various levels of preparation, and you will need to decide which level is necessary for the speech at hand. In this chapter, I want to share with you some of my own preparation techniques, and I am confident that you will be able to adapt and adjust my suggestions to fit your needs.

The PPQ

When I commit to speak before an audience, I ask the client to complete my Pre-Program Questionnaire (PPQ). Every professional speaker I know has a similar questionnaire, and veteran speakers will agree with me that this is one of the key elements to delivering a successful presentation.

My PPQ gives me a lot of basic and important information about the program itself and the logistics of the speech, as well as an overview and some general background knowledge of the group I am going to address. Here is a sample of the questions I ask on my PPQ:

I. The Program

A. What is your program theme?
   What does the theme mean to your group?

B. What kind of meeting will this be? (awards banquet, annual meeting, etc.)

C. What is the name and title of Dr. Alessandra's introducer?

D. Exact times of Dr. Alessandra's presentation:
   •Starting time
   •Ending time

E. What events take place immediately before and after Dr. Alessandra's presentation?
   •Before
   •After

F. What is Dr. Alessandra's role in the program? (Opening, closing, keynote, luncheon speaker, etc.)

G. Who are the other speakers on the program, if any?
Speaker	Topic	Day/time
Speaker	Topic	Day/time

H. What speakers have you used in the past?
Speaker	Topic
Speaker	Topic

I. What did you specifically like or dislike about the performance of speakers you have used in the past? Why? (Feel free to withhold names and only comment on their work.)

J. What ideas or skills do you want your group to retain from Dr. Alessandra's presentation?

K. Are there specific issues Dr. Alessandra should be sure to address?

L. How will you judge the success of the program when it is over?

II. Logistical Information

A. What is the nearest major airport to the meeting site?
   • Distance in miles to the meeting site
   • Distance in time to the meeting site

B. For transportation from the airport to the meeting site, would you prefer:
   • To meet Dr. Alessandra at the airport? Where?
   • To have Dr. Alessandra take a cab? Approximate cost?
   • N/A (local meeting)

C. Exactly where is the meeting?
   • Hotel
   • Address
   • City   State   Zip
   • Telephone   Fax
   • Meeting room number
   • Key contact at hotel

D. If Dr. Alessandra has any problems/emergencies on his way to the program, who should he contact? (Please include business and home telephone numbers)
  • Name
  • Business Phone   Home Phone

III. Audience Analysis

A. Audience
  • Number attending
  • Are spouses invited?
  • Percentage of males/females
  • Average age of group?   Range of ages?
  • Educational background of audience

B. What are the job titles of those in the audience?

C. Will there be any people in the audience who do not fit the description above? If so, please explain.

D. Are there any special people or guests in attendance? If so, who are they?

E. Toward which group should Dr. Alessandra primarily direct his presentation?

F. Describe the current *attitude and spirit* of:
  • A typical member of your group
  • Your firm or organization
  • Your industry

G. What are the main opportunities/challenges your organization currently faces?

IV. General Background Information

A. What industry is your company a part of? (circle one)
[list of industries]

B. What are the three key things Dr. Alessandra should know about your group?

C. Is there any jargon Dr. Alessandra should be familiar with (acronyms, etc.)?

D. Is there a phrase or common executive saying that may be effectively used by Dr. Alessandra in his presentation?

E. On which target markets/industries does your organization primarily focus for business?

F. Who is your typical customer? (C.F.O, Vice President of Human Resources, Purchasing Agent, etc.)

G. What is the primary product/service that you sell?

H. What kind of year did your group have last year? What are this year's expectations?

I. Any additional comments or information that would be helpful in tailoring this presentation to this group?

As you can easily see from the scope of my PPQ, I know a lot about a group before I ever see the faces in the audience. The PPQ is an invaluable research tool in helping me determine the focus of my speech, in actually writing the speech, and in establishing rapport with the audience once I arrive at the meeting site.

The client phone call

Once I receive the completed PPQ from a client, I call the client to discuss answers to the questions. This call often yields in-depth information or clarification that was not conveyed in the client's written responses on the PPQ. Frequently the client does not fill in every question or provides very short answers. The follow-up phone call helps fill in the blanks.

I sometimes ask for the names of three representative audience members that I might call to get a feel for the issues facing them. When I talk to the audience members prior to my speech, I bounce off them the key points of the speech I am preparing and ask for their feedback. I particularly ask, "How do you think the audience would respond to this point...this idea...this example...this joke...this story...etc.?" You would be surprised at how much good feedback you will get on these calls—feedback that may prompt you to cut, add, shrink, or expand what you had planned to deliver. Without this valuable feedback, you could be totally off the mark in your remarks. Unfortunately, that has happened to me—and I've learned from my mistakes.

Plan for an on-site meeting

It is always a good idea to visit with the client and your introducer when you arrive at the meeting site. Here you'll learn what has already taken place in earlier sessions at the meeting. What is the mood of the audience? What key issues have come up at previous sessions? What did previous speakers cover? How well did their material go over with the audience, and why? Has anything interesting or funny happened that you can build into your speech?

Room and A-V

In order for me to feel well-prepared and comfortable, I consider the room and audio-visual setup on a equal level of importance with having written and practiced my speech in advance. Room preparation is not unlike the relationship between the ambience in a restaurant and the food served—both are crucial to the total dining experience. Here's a sample of the audio-visual checklist I send to the meeting planner prior to my speech:

Room and A-V checklist

1. Preferred room setup
   - Theater style for more than 200 attendees or for short presentations
   - Classroom style for less than 200 or for presentations longer than 2 hours
   - Rounds for speeches in the same room as a meal function
2. Staging

   Because Dr. Alessandra is at his best when he is as close as possible to the audience, he prefers a T-shaped platform with a "runway" extending right up to the first row of the audience. This is very important to facilitate the way he works with the audience.
3. Lighting

   Dr. Alessandra prefers the house lights up as high as possible, except for the lights directly above the screen, which should be unscrewed. He moves around a lot as he speaks, beginning in the center of the room and moving closer to the audience. The audience should be able to see him clearly, and he them.
4. Audio-visual materials
   - Wireless (tie-clip) microphone perferred. (Second choice: lavaliere with 50 foot cord)
   - 35 mm projector and screen for Dr. Alessandra's horizontal, glass-mounted slides, with a wireless remote control
   - If using a rear-screen projection, screen can be placed anywhere
   - If using a front-screen projection, place screen at front corner (left or right) of room
   - Please do not place screen in center of room

Even though I send this A-V checklist to every meeting planner I work with on a presentation, the room is seldom set up totally to my specifications when I arrive. That's why it is imperative to do an in-person room check prior to your speech and before any of the audience is in the room. Be particularly certain that you check the staging (platform or podium placement, etc.), the lighting (how well are you lit? Does the lighting prevent the audience from seeing the screen if you are using slides, overhead transparencies, or video?), the microphone (particularly if it is wireless), and A-V equipment (35 mm projector, slides, video, etc.)

Remember: Room or A-V glitches can ruin an otherwise great speech!

Researching your topic and client

When I first began speaking in the early 1970s, I had to do all my research at the library. It was a tedious process. Not everything I needed on a topic or a client was at my library, so I oftentimes had to partake of interlibrary loans that took days to reach me—sometimes not in time for my speech.

Today, things are very different. Now you can do most of your research, if not all of it, "online" with a computer and a modem. One of the experts in this new field is Wally Bock, a consultant and the author of *Cyberpower!* He recommends the ABI/Inform database, a source that provides international coverage of more than 800 journals on banking, insurance, real estate, accounting and finance, marketing, data processing, and telecommunications. This database includes informative abstracts which summarize the contents of the original article.

Many magazines and newspapers are now available online, including *TIME, The Chicago Tribune, The New York Times, The New Republic, U.S. News and World Report, Scientific American, Industry Week, Wired,* and many more. There are clipping services available online that will scan news wires and publications for you and select stories based on a profile that you select—for example, the name of a client (IBM, AT&T, Time Warner, etc.) or a topic (sales automation, quality circles, interstate banking, etc.). Wally Bock recommends the following:

1. HeadsUp. Delivers custom news to your e-mail box or fax machine every business day.
2. Executive News Service. On CompuServe. Clips stories with key words you select from selected news wires.
3. Newshound. On America Online. Clips news stories based on your criteria.

Several databases exist online that you can use to get ideas for a topic, do your research, or gather great up-to-the-minute examples. Here's a list to get you started:

- A-V Online: Information on all non-print media (films, transparencies, videos, slides, etc.) covering all levels of education.
- ABI/Inform: Business practices, corporate strategies, trends.
- Academic Index: General interest, social sciences, and humanities literature with an emphasis on academic journals.
- America: History and Life. Wide range of information on U.S. and Canadian history.
- Books In Print: Currently published, forthcoming, and recently out-of-print books.
- BusinessWire: Unedited text of news releases from over 10,000 U.S. organizations and corporations.
- ERIC: Research reports, articles, projects significant to education.
- GPO Publications Reference File: Publications for sale by the U.S. Superintendent of Documents.
- Harvard Business Review: Complete text of this important business publication.
- Historical Abstracts: Article summaries of the history of the world from 1450 to present.
- Legal Resource Index: Index of over 750 law journals and reviews.
- Life Sciences Collection: Coverage of research in biology, medicine, biochemistry, ecology, and microbiology.

- Magazine Index: Index to articles in over 400 general interest U.S. magazines.
- Marquis Who's Who: Detailed biographies on nearly 75,000 professionals.
- PAIS International: Broad-based source for all areas of public policy.
- PsychoINFO: Leading source of published research in psychology and behavioral sciences.
- Public Opinion Online (POLL): Comprehensive collection of public opinion surveys conducted in the United States.
- Quotations Database: Omnibus file of literary, political, and other quotations of note.
- Sociological Abstracts: Worldwide coverage of sociological research.
- Standard & Poor's Corporate Descriptions: Information and news on over 12,000 publicly-held U.S. Companies.
- Standard & Poor's News: Financial news on U.S. public companies.
- Standard & Poor's Register-Biographical: Information on approximately 72,000 key business executives.
- Trade and Industry Index: Indexes of popular general business publications and industry trade journals.

Electronic information is a rapidly evolving field, and by the time you have this book in your hands, it is likely that there will be hundreds of new resources available. I recommend that you consider hiring a consultant–as I have hired Wally Bock–to help you be more effective online. If you would like to reach Wally, you can e-mail him at wbock@cyberpower.com (no period at end of e-mail address).

Preparation precedes success

One of the biggest mistakes non-professionals make when giving a speech is not being well prepared–"winging it," as some like to say. Every successful speaker who has contributed to this book will tell you that "winging it" is usually a sure-fire prescription for ineffectiveness on the part of the speaker and disappointment on the part of the audience.

Start preparing for your speech as early as possible, even though it may be weeks of months away. Waiting until the last minute could be devastating to the success of your speech and boring to your audience. Preparing for your speech well in advance and taking the steps I've recommended to help you get to know your audience and the meeting site well should give you a head-start on the road to speaking success.

A former graduate professor of marketing, Dr. Tony Alessandra combines powerful content with electrifying delivery in his professional presentations. Since 1976, he has delivered nearly 2,000 presentations, authored 11 books, and been featured in over 50 audio/video programs and films. His programs focus on his integrated approach to marketing, sales, and service, which show how to outmarket, outsell, and outservice the competition; how to sell value in order to turn targeted prospects into profitable, long-term customers; and how to get others to do what you want by giving them what they want. Topics on which he frequently speaks include "People Smarts," "Moments of Magic," "Collaborative Selling," and "The Power of Listening." Dr. Alessandra is also the owner of a sales automation software company.

Customize Your Style and Content To Fit Your Audience

10

Jim Cathcart, CSP, CPAE
P.O. Box 9075
La Jolla, CA 92038
619-558-8855
800-222-4883
Fax 619-558-9677
On line: jecathcart@aol.com

The quickest way to bond with an audience is to customize your message and delivery to the people you are addressing. It's also the quickest way to get the butterflies out of your stomach.

When your audience feels that you understand their interests and concerns, that you have taken the time to learn about them, that you *care* about them, they develop rapport with you. Customizing your message helps overcome skepticism and hostility. Members of your audience cooperate more fully and are more receptive to your message because their trust level is higher.

When you customize your message, your audience warms up to you sooner—and you get the butterflies under control sooner. You can actually feel the audience's good will. Your humor works better, and your ideas hit home more quickly. You gain confidence.

Customizing delivers big rewards, and it is not difficult to do either. In fact, a little effort in customizing goes a long way toward connecting with people.

Critical elements in customization

There's a universal answer to all questions concerning how to customize a talk: "It depends."

Six critical elements of a speech can be customized, and there are five levels of customization. How you combine the elements and levels depends on your goals for the speech and the amount of energy you can devote to customizing it.

1. The event itself often can be altered to create a desired effect. For example, you can make the presentation longer to permit more audience involvement. You can change the theme of the meeting to better match your desired message, or you can change your message to match their theme.

2. The people. You can invite different participants, depending on your desired outcome. Or you can refer to and involve certain individuals to help make a point.

3. The time. You can refer to the time, date, holiday, or significance of this time for this message. Or change the timing of your speech to occur strategically before or after some key event.

4. The place. You can use the location or its attributes to drive home your point or to establish a common reference with the group. Or you can shift the speech to a location that would have a more useful effect on the message.

5. The circumstances. If it is hot or cold, crowded or wide open, use that in your speech. Note any news item that is on everybody's mind and use it.

6. The speaker or message. Use something unique about yourself as a point of reference. Or show how your message itself is vitally important to the members of your audience.

All of these items lend themselves to adaptation within your speech. How and where you use them depends on how well they fit your purpose.

Levels of customization

As I mentioned previously, there are five levels of customization, each of which requires a fuller understanding of the audience. The levels are:

- Acknowledgement
- Reference
- Illustration
- Involvement
- Integration

The level you choose depends upon your goals for the presentation and the uniqueness of the situation you and the audience are in. The more you hope to accomplish through this speech, the more fully you will need to customize it.

My experience leads me to suggest that you not attempt to change the message you have to convey, but rather change the way you convey it, to be more appropriate to the group. Change it to the level that suits the situation.

The first level of customization is *acknowledgement.* All this really requires is that you pay attention, acknowledging the person, the time, the place, the date, etc.

Let me give you an example. At a recent speech to a group of professional speakers, the following introduction was read:

Jim Cathcart, CSP, CPAE, is a veteran National Speakers Association member. He joined in 1976, was elected to the Board of Directors in 1980, was Convention Chair in 1982, and served as National President in 1988-89. In 1993, he received the Cavett Award. In addition to almost 20 years of full-time international speaking, there is another side to Jim. He has also been a bartender, a nightclub singer, a truck driver, a motorcycle salesman, a bill collector, a banker, an insurance agent, a behavioral scientist, and a business owner. He may not be able to hold a job, but he can certainly hold an audience. Let's welcome...Jim Cathcart.

I wrote that introduction as a way of customizing my talk to fit that particular audience. The introduction gives my credentials in context and tells why I'm significant as a speaker to that group. It tells about my experience as a speaker and then, to throw in a little humor, it tells about all those jobs I had over the years.

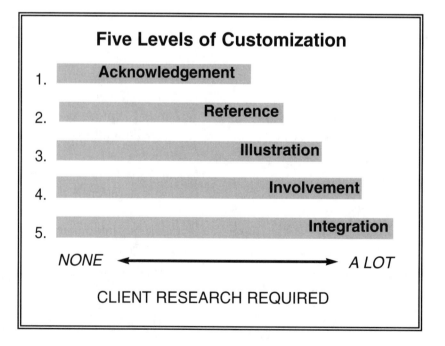

The typical response from an audience is: "This guy can't hold a job!" So I anticipated their response and built it right into the introduction script: "He may not be able to hold a job (pause) but he can certainly hold an audience. Let's welcome...Jim Cathcart." I've found that's a fun way to introduce a talk. And it gives me the opportunity to go in almost any direction I want.

My response to that introduction was, "Thank you for that introduction, Jean. It is exciting to be back before the *National Speakers Association* at this fifteenth annual meeting here in *Scottsdale.*"

I wrapped all of those "acknowledgements" together into a quick little statement at the first of the talk. When you do this, it's a gesture of caring toward the audience to show you know where you are, you know who they are, and you know what the circumstances are. What kind of client research is required for such acknowledgement? Almost none! You just have to pay attention to what is going on around you.

Reference is the next level of customization. Reference requires more research in order to gain a basic understanding of what the audience does.

For example, many years ago, I was asked to refer to the theme of a conference in my presentation for a computer user's group. The theme of the conference was "Optimization and Application in Process Control." What a challenge! I had to figure out some way to weave that into a talk on "Rethinking Yourself."

First I spoke with my client at length in an attempt to determine exactly what that theme would mean to the people in that audience. Then I thought about the relevance of my topic to their field. Next, I chose the references I would make to their theme and their field in my opening comments. When I stepped up to the platform, I said this:

Good morning, ladies and gentlemen. Process control is a topic you know well as it applies to technology, but I wonder if you've thought about it in regard to psychology. The essence of developing people is applying a form of process control. Today I'll show you several models for Rethinking Yourself and others with an eye toward optimizing your potential. My focus will not be on theory but rather on application. In other words, "Optimization and Application in Process Control."

The meeting planner in the back of the room was smiling from ear to ear and applauding me. She said, "Yes, that's what I wanted!" But it sure took some creative thinking for me to figure out how to weave that one in. And I had to first discover what "process control" meant to the people in the audience.

Throughout your speech, you can use references to such items as their corporate motto or company mission, a mascot or logo, and certain products or unique qualities about their organization.

The next level of customization is *illustration*, which means using their products or their people to make your point. Illustration is a higher level of application.

Once when I was scheduled to deliver a speech in Toronto, Canada, Peter Urs Bender—a fellow speaker and Toronto resident—had briefed me in advance about the country, the local area, and some local personalities. Each of these tidbits found their way into my speech as an illustration of one of my key points or as an ad-lib. The effect on the audience was wonderful. They all commented on how well I understood and respected them. Here's what I did:

Since the Toronto Blue Jays had won the World Series twice, I knew local residents would be justifiably proud. I also figured that since their opponents had all been U.S. teams, it would be rare to refer to baseball as a Canadian sport. So I said, "It's nice to be here in the baseball capital of North America." They erupted in spontaneous applause. Later on, I mentioned that it made very good sense for us to be meeting here, since "Toronto" is an Indian word for "meeting place." When I was speaking of a business concept, I illustrated it with examples of Canadian business leaders. For humor, I told them of hearing a lounge singer do a rendition of "South of the Border...down *Michigan* way."

You can spice up any speech by using examples and individuals from your audience to illustrate your points. And your audience will be grateful for the courtesy.

The fourth level—*involvement*—requires far more client research than illustration. This level of customization probably has as much power as any of the things we do as speakers. You can use exercises, role plays, questions and answers, and action plans (which members of your audience fill out as you go through the presentation).

At one annual meeting, a professional speaker did a presentation to a 1,000-person audience. He got them on their feet, got them to respond to his questions out loud or by raising their hands, had them interacting with each other. He was doing that with 1,000 people at one time! There's no limit to the size of the group you can get involved. But the larger the group, the more fundamental your instructions will need to be.

The highest level of customization is *integration.* You integrate yourself, your topic, your presentation style, the audience, and their circumstances into one unit.

Integration requires the utmost in client research. It means you must know their world, as well as understand their products, the inner workings of their company, and their competitive situation. They need to see you as one of them, not an outside speaker. The way I recommend you learn what you need for effective integration is to study as many of their materials as you can, and then visit their people and locations.

My first professional speaking engagement was for a Kansas-based company that was celebrating its twentieth anniversary. My assignment was to conduct two short seminars on personal growth and interpersonal communication for a group of 90 people, including spouses. To help me prepare for the talks, the client sent me their anniversary newsletter. The newsletter contained a detailed history of the company and brief profiles of the 45 managers who would be in my audience.

Since this was my first big booking, I overcompensated through preparation. For 30 days, I left their newsletter on my coffee table, and each night I reread it casually. Because of this repetition, I soon came to know all of the managers by heart. I knew their hobbies, spouses' names, kids, alma maters, etc. I also thoroughly understood the history and philosophy of the company.

By the time I arrived on-site, I recognized faces and could converse with members of my audience as an old friend would. Our rapport was instantaneous!

You can do this too by simply thinking as a member of your audience rather than as an outsider addressing them. Then study all you can about them, and treat them as colleagues.

Client research materials

To get the knowledge you'll require for customization, always request copies of their company literature and the names of key people within their organizations. Ask them to send you company magazines, industry publications, flyers, bulletins, clippings, and newsletters.

Another good source of material for studying a client is orientation manuals. An orientation manual usually contains the company's history, philosophy, mission and structure, and descriptions of different departments. The employees might have read it on their first day, but they forgot it long ago. And if you happen to know it, the audience will think you are brilliant.

Another idea is to get product manuals and flyers. Then you'll know what products they offer, how they operate, and the terms they use to refer to their products. Is the tractor they are selling a

J31B? Well, then you shouldn't call it Tractor "A." Call it what they call it.

Also request any organizational charts and annual reports. These have the key players' comments on recent trends, the operating philosophy, what's going on this year, last year, and so forth. That sounds like a lot. But you really aren't required to study all of this stuff at one sitting. You can do it over a period of weeks, or just skim it for highlights if you're not customizing very much.

The pre-program questionnaire

The materials I've just suggested you utilize should be in addition to a pre-program questionnaire. This is an absolute *must* if you plan to reach the higher levels of customization.

For almost 20 years, I have used a questionnaire to gather the information I need about each speaking engagement. Here is what a pre-program questionnaire should contain:

•*Logistics.* Where and when will you speak? How will you get there and back? Who will be your contact? Where will you meet them? How will you know each other? Who do you contact in the event of an emergency?

•*Staging.* How will the room be set up? What audio-visuals will be available? Will other presenters require a different set up just before you?

•*Program.* When and for how long will you speak? Who introduces you? How should you dress? What's on the agenda just before or after you? How likely is the program to be on time?

•*Content.* What do they want your speech to accomplish? What change do you expect from the audience? Are there any touchy subjects? What is the overall meeting about?

•*Audience.* Who are they? What do they do? What else should you know about them? Who do they deal with most?

•*Background.* What speakers have they heard before? What

is happening in their field these days? What do they produce or sell? Who are their competitors?

I realize that this is a lot to ask for, but not knowing it can be hazardous to your speech. You may wish to gather the information by phone to cut down on the meeting planner's paperwork load.

The kind of research I've just outlined sounds like a great deal of work, doesn't it? Well, that's why speaking is such a powerful form of communication. Every detail counts.

As you review the material you've solicited, listen and look for:
• Terminology and jargon
• Typical situations
• Average-day scenarios
• Common problems
• Logos or slogans
• Attitudes and prejudices
• Anecdotes from them
• Their competitors (know what the competition is doing)
• Who they usually deal with (purchasing agents, computer operators, doctors, etc.)

The more you know about the group, the more everything works because you are able to relate your information directly to what they do. Even your ad-libs will work better if you really know the group.

Customizing before the event
Prior to your program, take responsibility for customizing the program announcements, any of your photos being used, the title of your talk, and the scripting of an introduction that is just right for that particular group.

Request a copy of each of the program announcements or

flyers they send out. You don't want the audience to be notified of things you're not aware of. It could be that someone misstates your topic. They could change one word and yet totally alter the expectations of the audience.

My strategy is to generate as much of the copy as I can myself. I want to write out what they're going to say about me. I'll personally write a little paragraph, or a couple of lines, that they can use in their materials. And I'll send them an introduction for me, or a bio that is specifically tied to the purpose of the meeting.

Customizing on-site

On-site begins the minute you leave your home to go to the engagement. I have driven to the airport, gotten on the plane, flown to my destination, then learned that the person standing beside me at the meeting registration desk sat near me on the plane all the way from San Diego. You never know when you've begun to make an impression on that group.

A good speaker arrives early and observes everything. Talk with the members of the group; talk with the new people; talk with the officers; talk with the hotel personnel; talk with everybody you can. You never know what you'll pick up that you might be able to use later.

Read the final program agenda, and get a copy of handouts. The material might say the meeting has been changed or the time has been shifted. Maybe you thought it was in Room A and now it's in Ballroom Z, or it's in a remote building and the people have to be bused there to hear your talk. On the final printed agenda given out at one meeting, I found to my shock that it showed that I was scheduled for two presentations, and yet I had only been booked to deliver one! Naturally some emergency adjustments were quickly made.

Next, meet and make friends with your introducer. A person once asked me, "How do you get your introducer to use the introduction?" First, put the person at ease. Recognize that most introducers are unfamiliar with their role and are often nervous about it.

Get to know the individual. Show respect. He or she has an important role—to create the initial mood you'll have to walk into. So if you are friendly and show respect, he or she will take that role much more seriously. If you are very demanding and use a lot of pressure, the introducer will resent it, and he or she may feel fearful. We all know the No. 1 human fear is getting up in front of a group. Knowing that, why should we put pressure on the introducer, someone who does not do this for a living?

You should make it as easy as possible to introduce you well. Your introduction should be short, written in big type, and have lots of space between the lines. Words should be easy to pronounce. And you should say to your introducer, "Please use it word for word. If you want to make some casual comments or have a little fun, please do it before you start the actual introduction. But once you get into this, please follow it, because my opening comments will relate directly to this written material." Most introducers will respect that.

Next, notice what the people laugh at. That means you must be there ahead of time. Pay attention. When they're listening to other speakers or talking among themselves, notice what sort of things they consider funny. You'll find that computer hackers find one thing funny; salespeople find another thing funny; and the two groups wouldn't even begin to understand each other's humor. Notice other reactions, too—such as sensitivities to particular subjects. Maybe there are some real taboos, some subjects you shouldn't be dealing with.

Listen to the previous speakers. Occasionally one speaker uses the same story, joke, or example as another speaker. You really need to hear the people before you, even if they are company people. Many times in-company people will have heard one of your speeches, forgot where they heard it, and decide to use your material in their speech.

Assume everyone you meet at the location is a member of the

organization, and treat them with respect. You never know—the guy in the hallway, the one who is there at baggage claim with you, the people down the street—they all may be in your audience.

A word of caution: Don't over-socialize. Some speakers think it is a great idea to really mix it up with the group and laugh and have a great time with them. I believe, if we are the person who is going to be on the platform later that day, our role is to stay relatively invisible, to be totally courteous and professional. Attend their events and show courtesy to them, listen to them and pay attention, but don't stand out. It's not your turn yet. Wait until it's your turn, and then stand out.

Customizing during the presentation

Capture the mood that is in the room and use it—either to change and to get rid of bad feelings, or to build, to go with the good feelings.

Keep the program on *their* time. If you were scheduled for 60 minutes and their program is 30 minutes overtime, don't take the full 60 minutes. Instead, help them get back on schedule.

If you have spent a great deal of time preparing, you may feel like saying, "Now wait a minute, you told me I'd get an hour, I'm taking my hour." But what you would be saying non-verbally is, "I really couldn't care less about this audience, or about you, the meeting planner. It's me who is important here." That kind of attitude will deny you opportunities down the road, as well as the respect of your audience right now.

Eliminate audience skepticism. If you know the audience is skeptical about you, give credentials in your introduction or in your opening moments that get rid of the skepticism. Involve them early and often. I like to walk right up to the platform and say something like, "Good morning, ladies and gentlemen. How many of you have been in this field for more than 10 years?" By asking them to raise their hands, it immediately gets involvement. This puts them at ease and gives me a sense of how responsive they are going to be. But be sure your opening question is very easy for them to answer; otherwise, you'll endure an awkward silence as they think about their answers.

If it is your topic they are skeptical about, cite sources and credentials. Give substance to your ideas.

Steps for customization

The more time and effort you put into client research before the program, the more chances you'll have to ensure that both the meeting planner and the audience are pleased with the results after your speech is over. These steps for customizing will lead to results that are consistently pleasing:

• First, define the purpose of your appearance. Why is it *you* were the person asked to speak?

• Select the appropriate level of customization, whether it is acknowledgement, reference, illustration, involvement, or total integration.

• Study the client. Do the appropriate amount of client research for the level of customization you have chosen.

• And finally, be appropriate to the situation and have fun. Let your natural style emerge by focusing on your audience's understanding of your message, not by focusing on your delivery. The way to show you care is by delivering a talk that fits your audience like a fine glove.

S ince 1977, Jim Cathcart has spoken before convention audiences of thousands and local gatherings of 10. He has been introduced by orchestras, singers, dancers, and pyrotechnics, and his introducer has failed to show up at all. After delivering 2,000 professional speeches, Jim has received the Cavett Award from the National Speakers Association, as well as the Council of Peers Award of Excellence (CPAE) and the Certified Speaking Professional (CSP) designation. He is the author of *Rethinking Yourself, The Acorn Principle,* and *Relationship Selling.* Known worldwide as a compelling thinker with a playful speaking style, he deftly tailors every talk to have maximum impact on his audience.

Setting The Stage For Success: A Before-You-Speak Checklist

11

Nido Qubein, CSP, CPAE
Creative Services, Inc.
P.O. Box 6008
High Point, NC 27262-6008
910-889-3010
Fax 910-885-3001

A young minister once asked his outspoken grandmother for a critique of his first sermon.

"I saw only three things wrong with it," she said, to her grandson's relief. "What three things were wrong?" he asked. Her answer dispelled his relief.

"First," she said, "you read it. Second, you didn't read it well. And third, it wasn't worth reading."

I hope you never face an audience as tough as the young minister's grandmother. But if you do, there are some things you can do to get ready for them. Later in this book, you'll find some excellent instruction on delivering memorable speeches. What I'd like to do is share with you some tips on important things to do *before* you set foot on the platform that can make every speech you deliver more successful.

Should you accept?

A good speech demands careful and creative preparation. The preparation should begin even before you decide to accept the invitation to speak. Your decision should be guided by the answers to these questions:

(1) Why should I speak to this audience in this place at this time?

(2) What should I speak about?

(3) How can I make it enjoyable, interesting, informative, and persuasive?

(4) How should I organize my speech?

(5) How can I prepare myself to make a good delivery?

(6) How can I keep calm and avoid stage fright during my speech?

(7) How can I connect with my listeners and keep them involved?

(8) What barriers to communication might I experience and how can I deal effectively with them?

(9) How can I clarify complex ideas, be convincing on controversial claims, and inject interest in otherwise dull material?

(10) How will I get the response I want from my audience, and how will I know when I get it?

Why you and why now?

The importance of Question 1 should be obvious. If you have nothing to say that will be useful or interesting to this group, then you shouldn't speak. If you are scheduled at a time and place and in a context that will make it difficult if not impossible for you to deliver your message effectively, then you should decline the invitation.

Before you accept, learn as much as you can about the organization that extends the invitation. Know its background, history, and purpose. If you accept the invitation to speak, will others interpret your acceptance as an endorsement of its goals? If so, are they goals you can comfortably endorse?

Find out about the interests of the people you've been invited to address. What do they already know about the things you speak on? What can you tell them that will add to their useful knowledge? How much time will you have in which to tell them?

Who else is on the program and what are their topics? In what order will they speak? How will your speech and your message fit into the overall program? Will you follow a dynamic or a boring speaker? Will the speech preceding yours be informative or inspirational?

Identify the barriers

Identify the barriers you may have to overcome to put your message across. Will this be a sympathetic, a hostile, or a neutral audience? Are you opening the program? Are you closing it? What kind of room arrangements will you find? Will you be the last speaker before lunch or the first after lunch? Will your audience come to you directly from a cocktail hour?

All these considerations are important in deciding whether this speech is likely to advance or retard your purpose. Don't go into a situation in which you know it will be hard to look good. If the deck seems stacked against you, pass.

Reasons to accept

With most invitations, you'll probably find plenty of good reasons to accept. Here are some good reasons for saying yes:

- You have some valuable information or insights you want to give to the group.
- Now is an appropriate time, and this is an appropriate place to share your insights with this audience.
- This audience will accept your leadership, provided you earn it when you speak.
- You have something important you want this audience to do.

Choosing a topic

Once you've decided to accept the invitation, your next task is to choose your topic. Here are some criteria for selecting a topic:

- It should be something you know about or can find out about.
- It should be a subject the audience knows something about but wants to know more.
- It should be timely and appropriate for the audience.
- It should be narrow enough that it won't be confusing.
- It should be instrumental in achieving the response you want.

Gather your materials

After you've chosen your topic, analyze what you already know about it and decide how much additional information you'll need. You're now ready to research your speech. Use the library, periodicals, your own files, and any other appropriate resources to fill in the gaps in your knowledge of the subject. Then, to make it truly your own speech, draw upon your personal experiences to provide vivid illustrations or use your imagination to produce original stories.

Organizing your speech

A lot of complicated formulas have been advanced for organizing speeches and other communications. It doesn't have to be complicated; it can be a simple matter of choosing the material you want to use and following your mind's natural selection process. Here's how I do it:

(1) I go through all my material and select only those points that are relevant to my audience and my speech.

(2) I write out one concise sentence that clearly tells what I'm going to say.

(3) I reduce my ideas to three or four sentences that clearly present the idea expressed in my topic sentence. I arrange

them in the most convincing order. This becomes my outline.

(4) I flesh out the outline with explanations, supportive statements, funny lines and stories, and persuasive points.

(5) I select a humorous, related story to use in my introduction and a brief summation of main points to use as my conclusion. I will end my speech with a clear, convincing challenge for specific action.

(6) I let it ripen in my mind and heart until I understand the implications of everything I will say, feel it very deeply, and am sure every point is as clear and convincing as I can make it.

Now I'm ready to deliver the speech in words that are spontaneous, but that spring from well-organized, deeply-felt thoughts.

Speech types determine preparation

How you prepare for a speech will depend on the type of speech you are called on to give. There are three basic types of public speeches:

(1) Impromptu
(2) Written text
(3) Extemporaneous

The impromptu speech usually is the most intimidating for the speaker, though it need not be. This is the speech you have to give on the spur of the moment, without benefit of notes or outline.

The need to respond with an impromptu speech may come when you're recognized from the platform at a public function and you're called upon for "a few appropriate remarks." It may happen at a board meeting when you're unexpectedly called upon to explain a project you're in charge of or a proposal you've made. Or it may happen when you're the program chairman for a service club meeting and the scheduled speaker fails to show.

Stay Calm

Considering that many people are intimidated at the thought of public speaking even when they have plenty of time to prepare, the impromptu speech causes serious concern for many. Two words are important to keep in mind in these circumstances: Don't panic!

If you are frequently called upon to speak on behalf of your company or organization, a good solution is to keep a generic speech on hand. This speech might contain your core message—the essence of what you want people to know about your organization. It should contain information that you're familiar with and don't have to look up. If you can't keep a copy of this speech in your briefcase, at least be familiar with its general outline, so that when you are called upon unexpectedly, you can quickly organize your thoughts.

When the call comes, take a moment to think. Make a quick mental outline of the points you want to make. Don't worry about the *words* you'll use; just organize the ideas. The words will come, just as the words come to you when you are engaged in ordinary conversation.

Extemporaneous and written speeches

Extemporaneous speeches are usually the most effective. By extemporaneous, I mean speeches for which you have carefully prepared an outline but then deliver your remarks without following a word-for-word written text. Your outline provides you with the ideas you want to express, but you then form these ideas into words in your natural, conversational way. This type of speech combines the advantages of spontaneity and good organization.

The written text is often preferred by non-professional speakers because there's a comfort level in having every word you expect to say written out beforehand. However, I have some special advice for working with written texts.

First, don't read from the text if you can help it. Use the text primarily as a guide to help you keep on track. Unless you are an excellent reader and something of an actor, reading a text will sound stiff and unnatural.

There are, however, some occasions when reading the text directly may be wise. When it's critically important that the information be delivered precisely and accurately, reading may be your only choice. If you are dealing with touchy legal issues, one stray ad-lib could cost you dearly.

Preparing a written text

As you write, remember that written language has one style and spoken language another. Write for the spoken language. Express your thoughts the way you would express them in a conversation, not the way you would write them in a letter or essay. Remember, too, that the eye can glide over words that stumble the tongue. Read the text aloud and make sure there are no tongue twisters and no difficult-to-pronounce combinations.

Instead of delivering the speech word-for-word, let your eye take in clusters of words so that your mind is dealing with ideas, not syllables. This will make it easier for you to express the ideas naturally and fluently.

A smooth, natural delivery will be easier if you are thoroughly familiar with the text. Don't try to memorize it, but know how it is organized and know what points you want to stress. You may want to underline the words you wish to emphasize and note the places you want to pause.

Thorough familiarity with the text will enable you to look up and maintain eye contact with the audience without fear of losing your place. If you do lose your place, don't worry. Calmly scan the page until you come to the right line. It will only take a moment, and you won't lose your audience.

When you use a speech writer

Speech writing is a communication specialty in itself. It is also time-consuming. Not all executives have the time or the inclination to devote to the craft. That's why corporations often have a staff of speech writers, or they delegate the task to members of their public relations departments.

Arranging to let someone else draft your speech can work fine, so long as the speech writer knows your thoughts and speech patterns. If the writer doesn't know you well, you could find yourself looking at a speech that distorts your viewpoint and uses a style of expression that is not natural for you.

The better a speech writer knows you, the better they can express your ideas in your kind of language. If the writer doesn't report directly to you, they should report to someone who knows you very well, and that person should edit the draft very carefully.

Here are some additional tips for working effectively with a speech writer:

• Make sure the writer has a clear understanding of your position on the issues you plan to address. If you have company literature or correspondence that states the official position, make it available to your writer. Your writer should have copies of corporate literature, including annual reports, sales and marketing literature, external and internal publications, and a file of executive speeches.

• When you come across articles or quotations that you find especially relevant or cogent, have your secretary clip them or copy them and send them to your speech writer.

• It will help the writer to have samples of your speaking or writing on hand. This can take the form of audio tapes, video tapes, speech manuscripts, and copies of correspondence. Such resources will enable the writer to familiarize himself or herself with your speech patterns and your word choices. If you have trouble pronouncing certain words or word combinations, the writer should know about it.

• A competent writer will provide you with a well-organized and well-written script. Your task is to personalize it. Never go to the platform with a speech you haven't read before.

• Take the time to read the draft while you are not rushed and are not distracted. Read the speech first for content. Has the writer included all the points you want to make? Is all the information factual? Does it express the viewpoint you want to express? Does it reflect your priorities?

Next, read the speech for style. Does the writer use any words that are unfamiliar to you, objectionable to you, or incompatible with your style of expression?

Then read the speech aloud. Do the words flow smoothly and naturally from your lips? Are there any tongue twisters? Are there any sentences that you can't speak in a single breath?

• Don't hesitate to second-guess your writer on the wording. This is your speech, and it should say what you want to say the way you want to say it. Make any word changes you think are necessary to make it conform to your natural form of expression.

As you read the speech, be alert for opportunities to add personal stories and anecdotes that will put your imprint on the speech. Stories and images add life, interest, and inspiration to your speech.

The Power of the Spoken Word

With all the technological wonders we can expect to enjoy in the twenty-first century, business executives will still find one of their most effective communication tools to be the one employed with great skill by Demosthenes 2,300 years ago: the art of public speaking.

In the years ahead, telecommunications will reach a widely-dispersed audience quickly and economically. Videophones and videoconferencing will make it possible to convey nuances of body language and facial expressions without being present. Fax machines and computer modems will allow messages to be sent quickly and recorded permanently. But none of these communications methods will equal the power of presenting the message in the flesh. They can't put communicator and audience in a shared ambiance. And nothing can stir the emotions like a live speech, eloquently crafted and superbly delivered.

A speech can be used to communicate your corporate vision, to guide employee motivation, to create a favorable image for your company, and to persuade public bodies to take action in harmony with the company's best interests. A public speech can exhort, entertain, explain, and persuade. People go back to their homes and offices and tell others what they have heard. The power of a good speech can be enormous and long-lasting. That is why the art of public speaking is well worth cultivating, and time spent in preparation for your next speaking engagement is likely to be time well spent.

N ido Qubein, CSP, CPAE, is one of America's most respected professional speakers and management consultants. He came to America with no money, no connections, and little knowledge of the English language, and went on to become a successful example of the private enterprise system. Today, he is chairman of Creative Services, Inc., and McNeil Lehman, Inc. He sits on the board of directors of a dozen corporate, educational, and national organizations including Southern National Corporation/BB&T, Northpointe Partners, High Point University, Mount Olive College, American Humanics Foundation, and the Economic Development Corporation. Nido speaks over 100 times a year on business, communication, selling, and leadership. He has authored many books, videos, and audio cassettes on these subjects. He holds numerous awards and distinctions including an honorary doctorate from his alma mater. His foundation grants some 30 scholarships annually to deserving college students.

Creative Storytelling: The Fine Art of Finding, Developing, Polishing, and Presenting The Story

12

Naomi Rhode, CSP, CPAE
SmartPractice
3400 E. McDowell
Phoenix, AZ 85008-3846
602-225-9090
Fax 602-225-0245

Have you ever been deeply touched by a speech or a presentation? Can you articulate what it was that moved you? Was it a concept that you took away with you? A thought that inspired you then and later? Was it a world condition presented in a way that you could not get it out of your mind?

It could have been any one of the above. But probably the message was moving and memorable because it was masterfully woven into the speech or presentation through the powerful art form of storytelling.

Whether your platform is public, business, professional, or personal, speaking is a privilege. You have been given the honor and the opportunity to influence, even to change, the lives of others. A story can help you convey your message in ways that no other speaking tool can. If you want to become the best speaker you can be—if you want to take full advantage of the wonderful privilege of the platform—you will work to master the art of storytelling.

Moments to remember

What is a story, really? Certainly it is more than pure facts. A story, well-told, has descriptive beauty and movement. It has power. It enables people to identify with something outside their lives that touches inside of them. A story has purpose. Sharing the music...plus the magic...plus the meaning...of a story can create a memorable moment for your audience.

As you think of storytelling as an art form and the magic meaning that you want to produce through sharing stories, place yourself in magical moments in your own life and extrapolate from them the stories that have changed you. Let me give you an example.

Maui, Hawaii is a place that has spawned memorable moments for my husband and me. Several years ago, we were walking along an isolated beach looking across the channel at the beauty of the island of Moloki, stretching its mountain peaks through puffy, capping clouds. We shared a bag of Maui chips, munching and crunching as we strolled and talked. Turning to take in some lovely view behind us, we noticed the beautiful pattern of the footprints we were leaving in the sand.

Moments later, a huge wave came rushing in, nearly wiping us off our feet. The potato chips bag flew from my hands, and the chips scattered. As I looked down, I noticed that the wave had totally obliterated our footprints from the sand.

I turned to my husband and said, "We didn't make much of an impression in the sand, did we?" Quickly but thoughtfully, he replied, "It was because we were not walking on high enough ground."

That little vignette of actual experience touched and inspired me then, as it still does today. I have taken that story and used it to turn an ordinary speech into a magical moment. You can do the same by taking your actual experiences, *your* stories, and presenting them personally with the passion of your experience.

Finding the story

You've prepared your speech or presentation. It is educationally sound, intellectually thought-provoking, and guaranteed to challenge change in your listener. But it lacks feeling; it has no soul; it lacks the emotion to move people. It lacks retainable substance, the "hook to hang on" that all good speakers know a presentation must have to be remembered. Where do you find the story?

Life is happening all around you. Stories are happening all around you. "The story" is watching life happen and meaningfully transposing and retelling those happenings.

There are several types of stories that you should begin looking for:

• *Biographical vignettes.* Other people's lives can provide vignettes to use in your speeches. One such story is Michelangelo's experience of painting the Sistine Chapel, lying on his back on a precariously high scaffolding, amidst the chill of Italy's winter, the paint dripping in his eyes, doing this at the elderly age of 88 because he had beauty in his soul yet to be shared with the world. This is an example of a biographical vignette that can be effectively retold to inspire your audience. Giving proper credit to the person who wrote the biographical sketch you use is of eminent importance.

• *Signature stories.* Developing a story which is "just your story" and can be told often, perhaps almost every time you speak, is the way to establish your signature story. To share someone else's signature story would be the worst case of plagiarism. What you want to find is a story that is extremely meaningful to you because it illustrates your life theme.

• *Created stories.* The use of our imaginations can result in a fun and fanciful type of created story. The once-upon-a-time type story can grab people's imaginations and let their fantasies complete the story in ways you had not dreamed of.

• *Classic stories.* These are the stories from the public arena which have been accepted and used over and over, but the original author is not known. The use of the words "the story is told of..." or "you've heard it said..." makes a point without plagiarizing when giving direct credit is impossible.

• *Poetic stories.* The use of certain poems in story form can be a very powerful way of sharing a point with your audience. Give credit to the author, of course.

• *Original stories.* One of the challenges I give myself professionally is to create an original story on the way to every speech I give. I take something that has happened within the last minutes or hours and translate that into a meaningful experience that I can share with the audience as I begin the speech. This focuses their attention on the relevance of the present and helps them to realize that what I am sharing with them is current.

Developing the story

Finally you have it—the perfect story! How can you be sure it has relevance and applicability? How do you "power punch" it?

• *Record and retain.* It's extremely important to keep a journal of your experiences to develop stories. Recording your stories is the way to remember and retain; later, you can review the story and see how it might be applied to a specific speaking opportunity.

Recently, a friend told me about her experiences with a "Park & Fly" business in a city in the East. It was a car park where customer service is an astonishment factor, not an expected factor. Here my friend was delighted with the availability of indoor parking, fuel, car wash, detailing, and fresh flowers for a take-home gift on her return. Every customer is offered coffee and a paper at no charge. All of these services are available for the same amount of money as is required for parking in other nearby car parks that offer none of the amenities.

The story my friend shared with me provided a real-life example of service excellence. Such a casual sharing of comments between friends can also provide material for you; the secret is to record the stories in a way that you can recall them and develop them for use with a specific client or in a specific presentation.

• *Analyze and intensify.* Once you have identified the specific story you want to use, it is important that you carefully analyze the factors of that story. Decide where you will intensify it to relay the emotional impact you originally experienced. Although editorial license may allow the amplification and/or exaggeration of a story, I choose not to alter facts. I only intensify and underscore the emotion of the story.

• *Create word pictures.* In telling the story, it is extremely important to create an irresistible word picture and perhaps a symbol that will burn in the minds of your audience. One of my signature stories is of an incredible trip to Zermatt.

In this story, I tell of the beautiful Kline Matterhorn Mountain which required two trams and a gondola to reach. I describe for my audience the shape of the mountain and the feelings I experienced on the tram on the narrow cable threaded into the distant black hole in the peak of that majestic mountain. If I am using handout material, I will even have them "doodle" the shape of the mountain as a memory keeper of that particular word picture I created. This is the preamble to the point of the story, creating attention and facilitating an application.

• *Apply and appeal.* Establish with your audience the meaning of the message, the purpose of the story, and how you think the story will benefit the audience. This is extremely important in storytelling. The story can be meaningful in even the most austere business setting if the listener knows and understands the purpose of the story. This purpose should be woven throughout the telling and emphasized at the end. The personal application—the life or behavior-changing appeal of the story—must be sufficiently obvious, or it may appear to be a waste of time for the listener.

• *Practice and polish.* At this point in the crafting of the story, the true art is applied. You look for and find words that encapsulate the significance of the story. The meaning rises from and transcends the facts of the story.

It has been my experience that practicing a story over and over verbally, sometimes as many as 15 to 20 times, is extremely beneficial.

Finding just the right phrases to express your thoughts, then finding the right way to say those words aloud, will assure a logical flow, enhance emotional impact, and help assure a meaningful, on-going application for the audience.

Adding meaningful body language solidifies the power of the story in the listener's mind. You can stimulate the listener's imagination to actually feel the heights of the mountain, the feelings of trepidation of the tram ride, the awe of the moment. Since 85 to 90 percent of everything we say is non-verbal, this portion of storytelling is extremely important. I believe it comes very naturally for some social styles and can certainly be learned and developed masterfully by others.

• *Own and master.* The stories you choose from your recorded repertoire must be poignantly poised to emphasize your entire message. The beauty of developing your own stories is that no one can tell them like you can. They are yours. You have experienced them. As you master them, they flow from your heart and your lips creatively with the music and art of your soul intertwined throughout.

• *Be the story.* You've probably heard the phrase, "The believable person is the one who walks their talk." In stories that are our personal experiences, our delivery is usually believable because our very being personifies the story.

Audience impact

What effect will your story have on your audience? Will there be tears in their eyes? Laughter in their souls? Celebration of life in their steps after being inspired by your words? Will the audience remember and share your stories, making your message part of their lives? The answer to how much impact your stories are likely to have will depend on several factors.

• *Appropriateness.* I believe the stories that have impact value the diversity of the audience without sacrificing its individuality. Research done ahead of time on who will be in the audience is extremely important. Knowing who we are sociologically, psychologically, and spiritually, and then interjecting our individual preferences is appropriate when it is not offensive to other people. Using a bit of sincere humor often helps to relay this kind of individuality without offending a diverse audience.

For example, in my description of Zermatt and the beauty of Switzerland, which is impossible to exaggerate, I can pause with a gesture, a twinkle, and a smile, and say, "I know the Person who made Switzerland." With lightness of spirit, I move on to the rest of my story quickly. This way, I maintain my individuality while still recognizing diverse beliefs in the audience. I have shared a brief insight into my spiritual beliefs, but in a non-offensive way. Without some personal distinctions, I believe there is a blandness to the presentation and an inappropriate vanilla approach to society and our world.

Early interacting with the audience before the session begins, eye contact and movement throughout the audience as you deliver the speech, and one-on-one interactions when you have completed the delivery can all help you develop a sensitivity to the appropriateness of your material for the audience you are addressing. On the other hand, an increasing awareness of the right of the individual to believe out of their experience and background is something that we as speakers must respect and protect. Certainly, customizing to group distinctions and respecting the philosophy of the particular group is a stamp of sensitivity and professionalism.

Within one three-day period, I spoke to corporation leaders in the chicken-growing industry, the Boy Scouts of America, and a group of dentists and their team members. In some instances, I used a story with one group and not another, but I shared several stories with all three groups. In each instance, I customized to group distinctions, considering the appropriateness for each group.

• *Timing.* I believe it is extremely important to respect the mood of the moment.

In 1993-1994, I served as president of the National Speakers Association. During the convention at the finale of my year as president, we received news of a tragic death in the family of one of our attendees. I was touched emotionally, and I was very involved in the comforting of this member as word of the event was conveyed.

Immediately after I heard news of the tragedy, I went to a luncheon attended by more than 1,800 members. It would have been easy to announce my concern for this person and encourage the audience to respond with cards and care. This would seem to be an appropriate gesture of empathy for one of our members. However, we were having two humorists make presentations at the luncheon. One of the humorists, I discovered, planned to share two stories that involved death. My announcement would have been extremely ill-timed.

In a sense, even an announcement is a story, and we must be careful to respect what has occurred prior to and what will occur after our presentation. Respecting the purpose of the meeting— i.e., educational, inspirational, growth, change, etc.—is also a guide to assuring impact through the correct timing of the stories we tell.

• *Emotional graphing.* As a young woman, I had the special privilege of being the organist in our church. Our minister was exceptionally effective at establishing the mood he wanted to create in the worship service. I worked closely with him on the kinds of music we would use at different points in the service to emphasize joy, praise, quietness, and prayer. Appropriate placement of stories is a similar art form. Actually, graphing our speeches and story placement is a wondrous art.

One of the challenges we face in emotional graphing is to recognize how we can use a story without crossing the line from "rejoicing the audience" to "raping the audience." Let me explain what I mean. I am sure you have heard people tell extremely tragic personal stories. I would encourage you as you are learning to be a more effective artist at storytelling to analyze other people's work and recognize when the story encouraged you in some way to be a better person, rather than crossing the line taking you to an unproductive depth of pathos.

Much of the difference in the way we tell the story again relates to our body language and our ability to go between humor, pathos, and tragedy with a sense of ease and movement. It is important to reassure our audience that we will not leave them down emotionally, but that we will again bring them up and send them out with a feeling of hope rather than despair.

Retention

To achieve the goal of changed lives comes from the sharing of "heart-stuff" vs. just "head-stuff." Heart-stuff is the content that causes change, heals, and causes people to envision preferred futures and interaction with others vs. probable futures.

I have a speaker friend whose 13-year-old son died in a skateboard accident. I have shared the letter she sent with her son's organs, which they donated so that someone else might live. It is truly a heart-rending letter that inspires people to seize the platform of opportunity in tragedy as well as in triumph. Yes, it is a heavy story in one sense, but it also is uplifting. Use of serious, thought-provoking material can be very effective when your goal is for retention and when you seek genuine change in your audience.

Another way to enhance retention is by using reminder "rhetoric" words and symbols that cause people to recall your presentation, as well as your story in the future. For my year as president of the National Speakers Association, I chose trumpets and roses in the logo to symbolize our theme of "The Privilege of the Platform." The trumpet is a wonderful symbol of the call to the platform, the call to professionalism, and the call to the clear message of the speaker. To me, the roses symbolize giving your very best to an audience and, of course, the best gifts are returned. It was my hope in creating the symbol that the membership of our association will never hear a trumpet blow or see and smell a rose without remembering the privilege they have of the platform.

Not only was the trumpet and the rose used in printed form during the year, but I used those symbols repeatedly in speeches and presentations that I made before NSA members and other groups. The trumpet and the rose became rhetorical reminders that triggered an immediate association at the very mention of the words.

Earlier in this chapter, I referred to a walk on the beach in Maui. I created word pictures as I described looking across the channel at Moloki while eating crunchy Maui chips. My description, if well executed, will cause people to remember that story when they think of Maui beaches, leisurely afternoons, footprints in the sand, mountains that snake through the clouds, and waves that grab Maui chips out of your hand. Retention reminders!

Certainly handouts, pictures, and cards with poetry all aid retention. And, repeating, repeating, repeating signature stories will cause the anticipation and even the demand to hear that story again and again. You can almost feel your audience saying, "Tell the story about...!"

Wrap-Around Stories

How can I "theme" an entire speech, seminar, or experience with a story? Does using such a story improve effectiveness and retention?

We have a seminar in Hawaii each January. I "play" with the audience the first day by sharing the idea that rain in Maui isn't really rain—it's pineapple juice. The sun always shines, the food has no calories—I create a list of how all's right with the world in Maui. I say with a twinkle in my spirit that "Macadamia nut ice cream with hot fudge sauce is a daily must!" Throughout the week, I return to that opening vignette and interject parts of it at unexpected times, calling it "Maui Magic." The audience's anticipation of my words—"Maui Magic", macadamia nut ice cream with hot fudge sauce", etc.—becomes so expected that audience members fill in the blanks for me without my having to say the words.

At that seminar in Hawaii every year, "Maui Magic" becomes a "wrap-around story," a theme and a fun factor. I have received many poems, stories, and anecdotes about "Maui Magic" through the years, and alumni will walk up to me and share that the macadamia ice cream with hot fudge sauce just doesn't "taste the same" at home. The "Maui Magic" wrap-around story has become the experience and the experience; has become "The Story."

Celebrate the privilege

It was 3:37 a.m, and the shrill ringing of the phone awoke me from a peaceful sleep in my bed at home in Phoenix, Arizona. Early on that August morning, a woman from the East Coast sobbed into the phone as she conveyed to me the news of her husband's death one hour before in a self-piloted small plane crash. They had both been in many of my audiences during their struggles for personal, marital, and professional success. And, they had accepted the challenges I made during platform and personal counseling sessions to be tenacious in striving for personal and interpersonal health. In the midst of her pain and tears, she said words that I treasure:

> "I will *never* be able to thank you enough for modeling,
> speaking, and sharing the challenge of a good marriage and
> professional excellence. Now I will be able to speak at
> Doug's memorial service with my head and heart high."

Her call was a gift, wrapped, and preciously presented, that reminded me over and over again of the power and privilege of the speaking platform.

Speaking is an art form, a means of communication, an articulation of thought, a form of persuasion, a powerful change agent, an educational facilitator. Whether your platform is public, business, professional, or personal, every speaking engagement is an opportunity to influence the lives of others. You have been chosen to model and articulate messages that can serve as change agents for members of your audience.

As a professional speaker, I always make sure that I ascend the platform knowing in my soul, with a burning fire, what I want to "have happen" as a result of my platform presentation. I know what I want the audience to think, learn, feel, retain, and change. I believe in the concepts thoroughly, present them creatively, and encourage them enthusiastically, believing that to do so can result in life-changing growth for members of my audience.

Are you giving a sales presentation, a nomination speech, a memorial presentation, an honor banquet announcement, an inspirational talk, a keynote, a consulting plan, a training session, or a seminar? Are you speaking (communicating) for the first time with a stranger or the ten thousandth time with a loved one? All these are speeches. All are privileges of your personal and professional platform. The difference between memorable impact and casual, non-retained happenstance will be magical, meaning-ful moments. I wish you many of those in every speech you make.

My father would often close one of his campfire chats with family, friends, or Boy Scouts with this little poem. It is bur-nished into my soul with the memory of fire crackling, marsh-mallows roasting, and fireflies flitting in cool, crisp Northern Minnesota evenings. It is the magic I'd like to leave with you:

The Value of Little Things
For want of a nail, the shoe was lost.
For want of a shoe, the horse was lost.
For want of a horse, the battle was lost.
For want of a battle, the kingdom was lost.
All for the want of a horseshoe nail.

Perhaps as we look at the power and privilege of our individual platforms, we can transpose this childhood poetry to the following:

For want of a moment of meaning, the message was lost.... Because of a story well-delivered, the platform privilege was won!

Naomi Rhode, CSP, CPAE, is a past president of the National Speakers Association and is known for her inspirational, dynamic speaking to both healthcare and general audiences. She shares her expertise with her audiences on team building, interpersonal communication, leadership, and empowerment. Each year she speaks extensively at seminars, association meetings and conventions, stimulating her audiences to achieve new levels of professional and personal growth. In addition to speaking, Naomi is the author of two inspirational gift books: *The Gift of Family—A Legacy of Love* and *More Beautiful Than Diamonds—The Gift of Friendship.*

Tools For The Master Speaker

13

Charles "T" Jones, CPAE
206 West Allen Street
Mechanicsburg, PA 17055
717-691-0400
800-233-2665
Fax 717-766-6565

Speaking is a wonderful profession because it combines a little of every profession. We are architects and builders helping people build a better life. We put windows in their thinking to help them see and think more clearly. We are doctors giving a shot of laughter to heavy hearts. We are chefs and dieticians, selecting the right ingredients and serving up appetizing food for thought. We are salesmen of ideas and ideals. We are farmers planting seeds and fertilizing minds. We are trainers, evangelists, and much more.

My speaking began 45 years ago, and my audiences have ranged from two to 50,000 on five continents. I have had many Tremendous experiences but none more wonderful than the constant discovery of new dimensions of old truths and learning anew that while speakers are teachers and evangelists, they are—even more—students and servants.

Even if you are not a professional speaker, you can taste a bit of the wonderful satisfaction speaking can bring every time you address an audience. And, as you increase your speaking skills, you will find that the satisfaction you gain from speaking increases also.

The one thing every profession has in common is tools. Every doctor, farmer, or builder couldn't operate or build without tools and the knowledge and experience to know which are the right ones and how to use them.

In this article, I would like to share with you some tools that have helped me become a better speaker. These may not be skills as specific as the ones you will learn about by reading the other articles in this book. They are, instead, traits you can develop in yourself and approaches to your work and your life that will make you a wiser person and, therefore, a more inspiring speaker.

The tools I will discuss are not all the speaking tools available, but I believe these would be high on every Master Speaker's list. They are tools that need not be bought; these are tools already inside of you that must be discovered, thought through, and worked out. Eventually, working them out will change to living them out.

In my early speaking apprenticeship, I attended the Presidential Prayer Breakfast and Seminar. Moorehead Wright of General Electric Company was one of the speakers. He made a statement which has demonstrated to me the power of speech for 40 years. He said, "Ninety percent of all growth is spiritual." Being young, ambitious, enthusiastic, and full of energy, that statement was made for me, and it is the only thing I remembered. This statement is the reason all the tools I've chosen to share with you are tools that will aid your 90 percent growth area.

"Thy soul must overflow
If thou another soul would reach;
It needs the overflow of heart
To give the lips full speech."
—Charles Spurgeon

Speaking tool #1: Books

"You are the same today as you'll be in five years except for two things, the people you meet and the books you read."

There are very few Americans who have not heard of Og Mandino and Earl Nightingale. The one thing they have in common, other than fame, is books. I think it is interesting that both read to share, not just to improve themselves. Earl Nightingale took the best of the motivational and inspirational classics and crammed them into an 18-minute record called "The Strangest Secret," which became the all-time best seller. Og Mandino reviewed thousands of books as editor of *Success Unlimited*, and then one day, all his reading and sharing evolved into the hugely-popular *The Greatest Salesman in the World*, which Og followed with many more classics.

I tell my audiences that for every point I make, I can tell them the books where I got the seed thought. I think John Wesley's letter in 1780 to a fellow clergyman will convince any speaker that books and reading are not an option:

"What has exceedingly hurt you in times past, now, and, I fear, to this day, is your want of reading. I scarce ever knew a speaker read so little. And perhaps by neglecting it, you have lost the taste for it. Hence your talent in speaking does not increase. It is just the same as it was seven years ago. It is lively, but not deep; there is no compass of thought; **only reading** can supply this, along with meditation and prayer. You wrong yourself greatly by omitting this. You can never be a deep speaker without it any more than a thorough Christian. O begin! Fix some part of every day for private exercises. You may acquire the taste which you have not. What is tedious at first, will afterwards be pleasant. Whether you like it or no, read and pray daily. It is for your life; there is no other way: Else you will be a drifter all your days, and a petty, superficial speaker."

We are reminded in every decade that we are living in changing times, but great books will remind you that the things that matter and the tools of the Master Speaker never change.

I recommend you read autobiographies and biographies. General Patton hit it right on the head in a letter he wrote to his son while waiting to go ashore on D-Day:

> "To be a successful soldier, you must know history. Read it objectively—dates and even minute details of tactics are useless. What you must know is how man reacts. Weapons change, but man, who uses them, changes not at all. To win battles, you do not beat weapons—you beat the soul of enemy man...You must read biography and autobiography. If you will do that, you will find that war is simple."

I began using my "Books you read..." quote over 30 years ago. Today, thousands are quoting it and giving me credit. I found almost an identical quote in a book written over 100 years ago. The things that matter never change.

Speaking tool #2: Humility
"Humility is the first test of a great man."—John Ruskin
"Don't be so humble; you are not that great."—Golda Meir

I remember hearing a speech over 40 years ago by Tom Watson, who was the president of IBM and who, at that time, was the standard of excellence in everything. His opening remark was on how he reached the top. He smiled and said, "I was born the son of the founder..." I would have been impressed with his message regardless of that statement, but his humility touched me.

One of the Master Speaker's greatest tools, and one that you should keep in mind as you prepare and deliver every speech, is humility. This quality will shape and flavor your every word and idea. A great illustration of this point is the young seminarian who was zealously planning his first sermon. He had written and rewritten his great sermon on what was wrong with the world, and he had all the answers. He continued to rehearse and prepare for the big day when the congregation would see how good he was.

Well, the big day arrived. He proudly marched to the pulpit and began to deliver his message. Almost immediately, he realized that being in the pulpit, with all the eyes staring at him, was quite different from reading in front of a mirror. In a few minutes, he began to realize that he was in trouble; he began to panic, and his throat became dry. His heart was pounding; the sweat began to come; he began to wish there was a trap door behind the pulpit and a push button that would allow him to drop out of sight. But there was no trap door or push button, so he said a hasty benediction.

Beaten, discouraged, dejected, head hanging down, he left the platform. As he walked the aisle, an old-timer slipped his arm around his shoulder and whispered in his ear, "Son, had you gone up like you came down, you could have come down the way you went up."

I think I've lived this illustration a thousand times. It is good to realize humiliation can be a good experience if you accept it in the right spirit. If you don't, you will find arrogance will take the place of your humility. If this does happen to you, don't worry; a dose of honesty, and your humility will be on the way back.

"If a man's faults were written on his forehead, he would draw his hat over his eyes."—Anonymous

"It's easy to be humble if you are honest."—CEJ

Speaker's tool #3: Enthusiasm

"Enthusiasm is to the personality what steam is to the locomotive, the power that produces action."—Montapert

"Every product of genius must be the production of enthusiasm."—Disraeli

John Wesley was asked how he attracted such crowds. He replied, "I just set myself on fire and people will come from miles around to watch me burn." I first heard this quote from Hall Nutt, Director of the Purdue Life Insurance Marketing Institute. He was a perfect example to tell the story because he was totally uninhibited. He was constantly smiling, laughing, moving, waving his arms and dramatizing a point. For example, in speaking to a group of insurance agents, he would throw slices of bread into the audience to remind them that even though dollars are necessary to buy insurance, it's the food that families need. You never forgot after that demonstration that you were selling food, not insurance.

Frank Bettger is probably responsible for saving more sales careers than any other person because of his speeches and books on enthusiasm. Here's how he described the power of enthusiasm in his book on success in selling.

"My whole life might have been different if I hadn't gone to the manager and asked him why he fired me. In fact, I wouldn't have the rare privilege of writing this book if I hadn't asked him that question.

"The manager said he fired me because I was lazy! Well, that was the last thing I expected him to say.

"You drag yourself around the field like a veteran who has been playing ball for 20 years,' he told me. 'Why do you act that way if you're not lazy?'

"'Well, Bert,' I said, 'I'm so nervous, so scared, that I want to hide my fear from the crowd, and especially from the other players on the team. besides, I hope that by taking it easy, I can get rid of my nervousness.'

"'Frank,' he said, 'it will never work. That's the thing that is holding you down. Whatever you do after you leave here, for heaven's sake, wake yourself up, and put some life and enthusiasm into your work!'

"I had been making $175 at Johnstown. After being fired there, I went down to Chester, Pennsylvania, in the Atlantic League, where they paid me only $25 a month. Well, I couldn't feel very enthusiastic on that kind of money, but I began to *act* enthusiastic. After I was there three days, an old ball player, Danny Meehan, came to me and said, 'Frank, what in the world are you doing down here in a rank bush-league like this?'

"Well, Danny,' I replied, 'if I knew how to get a better job, I'd go anywhere.'

"'A week later, Danny induces New Haven, Connecticut, to give me a trial. My first day in New Haven will always stand out in my memory as a great event in my life. No one knew me in that league, so I made a resolution that nobody would ever accuse me of being lazy. I made up my mind to establish the reputation of being the most enthusiastic ball player they'd ever seen in the New England League. I thought if I could establish such a reputation, then I'd have to live up to it.

"From the minute I appeared on the field, I acted like a man electrified. I acted as though I were alive with a million batteries...The newspaper began calling me 'Pep' Bettger—the life of the team.

"I mailed the newspaper clippings to Bert Conn, manager of Johnstown. Can you imagine the expression on his face as he read about 'Pep' Bettger, the dub he'd tied a can to three weeks before—for being *lazy?*

"Within 10 days, enthusiasm took me from $25 a month to $185 a month. It increased my income by 700 percent! Let me repeat: Nothing but the determination to act enthusiastic increased my income by 700 percent in 10 days! I got this stupendous increase in salary, not because I could throw a ball better, or catch or hit better, and not because I had any more ability as a ball player. I didn't know any more about baseball than I did before."

There is no word more misunderstood or misused than this Tremendous word **enthusiasm**. Many equate enthusiasm with being an extrovert. Nothing could be further from the truth. Enthusiasm is that fire that can burn in every heart and word, if the fire is lit and fueled. There is nothing more beautiful than a soft-spoken grandmother talking about her grandchildren. No one need give her a book or speech on how to act enthusiastic when talking about her grandchildren. Just give her a listening ear and keep your mouth shut, because her inclination to be an introvert will be forgotten as something far greater than being concerned with "What will people think?" takes control of her personality.

We have heard and read the great truth, "Act enthusiastic and you'll be enthusiastic." I heard it, believed it, practiced it, and repeated it; but I'm glad I discovered there are two sides to every question and many dimensions of truth.

I now realize that if you act enthusiastically long enough, you can fall in love with your act and your fellow actors will be your only admirers. We need to be learning in our early stages that we need to do a little acting, but hopefully, through our failures and successes, we begin to focus our attention on the needs and problems of others and the real enthusiasm that flows Above-Down-In-Out Service will begin to allow us to enjoy *being* enthusiastic so that we can quit just *acting* enthusiastic. When you're *acting* enthusiastic, the emphasis is on you; when you're *being* enthusiastic, the emphasis is on others. Living it out is always better than acting it out. Remember: Acting enthusiastic is always better than the living death portrayed by many.

Speaking tool #4: Laughter
"The most wasted of all days is that one in which one has not laughed."—Camfont

There is one fact that will help keep the speaker's feet on the ground while he soars with the eagles: Young and old, rich and poor, sick and healthy people have something in common. They all experience hurt. Some hurts you live through and some you live with, but no one gets through life without some hurts. Some are self-inflicted, and some are imaginary. But regardless of the cause, they are a part of life. Most listeners know that a speech can't take away their hurts, but they can experience some relief and even see the positive side of hurt through the Tremendous tool of laughter.

I remember reading in the newspaper about the death of a popular young comedian, Freddie Prince, who took his own life. The story said as Freddie's heart stopped beating, a young nurse fell on his chest, beating on his heart, sobbing, "Please don't die, Freddie. The world needs all the laughter it can get." Perhaps the most-loved and best-known comedian is Red Skelton. I enjoy him even without seeing or hearing him because he is part of every life that he has made laugh.

A speaker can use the laughter tool in a more meaningful way than a comedian. The comedian tells jokes to get people to laugh at him or the joke. The Master Speaker will use humor to get his listeners to laugh at themselves or see a truth.

Laughter never solves the problem, but it helps us to live with it, grow through it, and build on it.

Speaking tool #5: Energy

General Patton said, "You can never grow until you push yourself past the point of exhaustion." What a Tremendous truth! You'll never discover how much energy you have until you use what you have and put yourself in a situation where you have to draw on energy you didn't know you had.

Oswald Chambers said, "If you spend yourself physically, you'll become exhausted; but if you invest your life spiritually, you'll draw new strength." Another Tremendous truth!

I remember an experience years ago that I am sure I'd never do again, but it was a Tremendous lesson for me. I was doing all I could to book any meeting, anywhere, anytime. First, I booked a luncheon in Winnipeg and a real estate seminar the following morning in Detroit. Soon after those bookings were confirmed, I had an invitation for a dinner meeting in Montreal and another in Honolulu. I knew it was all but impossible to fly 10,000 miles and speak at four meeting in 24 hours, but being desperate for every meeting, I thought I'd take a look. Because of the time changes between Montreal, Winnipeg, and Hawaii, I was able to make each meeting, get the 11:30 p.m. flight from Hawaii, and be ready to go to work at 10:00 a.m. the next day in Detroit. Some might say that was insane, but I was young, naive, ambitious, and had six hungry children. I also had the satisfaction of pushing myself past the point of exhaustion, and the realization of a truth that has to be lived out, not thought out.

Speaking tool #6: Preparation

"If I had eight hours to chop down a tree, I'd spend six sharpening my ax."—Abraham Lincoln

Every speaker knows the importance of self-confidence and some, through self-hypnosis or self-affirmation, can convince themselves that they are confident, and even project it. But there is something far better: **Preparation**.

Self-confidence without preparation will erase those wonderful qualities of sensitivity, empathy, and compassion. You will be speaking at people instead of thinking with them. Preparation allows your delivery to flow, and your audiences to be at ease. And your audience will be at ease when they sense you are at ease.

One of my first talks was to our GIs. The Gideons were giving them a luncheon and a Bible before they went off to Korea. Because of my youth and enthusiasm, I suppose, they selected me to give a 10-minute message. I was humbled by the invitation because I knew that every member was better qualified than I to deliver inspirational words. So this motivated me to spend 18 hours preparing my 10-minute talk. You might think that put me at ease, but it didn't. My knees still shook, but at least I had a well-prepared message and plenty left over for the next 10 talks. I also began learning that preparation has to be followed by practice. After many failures and a few successes, you settle down and your audience follows your lead.

Preparation is to help you know what you know and know you know it. Preparation will help you see the importance of being narrow instead of broad. When you are broad, you know a little about a lot. You are a mile wide and an inch deep. When you are narrow, you know a lot about a little—but what you know, you *know* you know and your audience will sense you know.

Speaking tool #7: Wisdom
"Wisdom is knowing what to do next."—Jordan

For the Master Speaker, wisdom is knowing what is worth saying and saying it. Sometimes reading a speech can have just as much impact as hearing a speech.

Roger Hull, one of my first role models, gave me a copy of a speech by Edward Hanify, an attorney who delivered a speech, "Leadership and Exalted Trust," at a legal convention. His closing words became a part of my life and many of my speeches. "A man," Hanify said, "can be born with ability. He can acquire knowledge. He can develop skills. But wisdom comes only from God."

I have over 200 biographies on the life of Lincoln. My love for Lincoln began at Gettysburg, where I bought a plaque which has hung in my office for over 40 years. It says, "I must confess that I am driven to my knees by the overwhelming conviction that I have nowhere else to go. My wisdom and all about me is insufficient to meet the demands of the day."

There are no schools that can grant a degree in wisdom. Even the intellectual elite know that wisdom isn't reserved for any particular group or person. Wisdom is reflected in the life of one who feels they owe much and deserve little. Wisdom always manifests itself in *an attitude of gratitude*.

In my youthful ignorance, I would say no one gave me anything—I earned it. Now that I've experienced a little wisdom I can say that all I have that matters, I was given. Therefore, my success can never be a reward to be enjoyed, but rather a trust to be administered.

Speaking tool #8: Heroes—Someone to look up to

"Heroes are those who have changed history for the better. They are not always the men or women of highest potential, but those who have exploited their potential in society's behalf. Their deeds are not done for the honor, but for the duty. Through our study of heroes, we enter the realities of greatness."—Fred Smith

Wherever I look in my office, I can see a picture of one of my heroes. Here are 10 of my many heroes; I owe them everything: The Apostle Paul, Abraham Lincoln, Robert E. Lee, Milton Hershey, Oswald Chambers, General Patton, David Livingstone, Patrick Henry, Sam Houston, and my father.

Speaking tool #9: Role models—Someone to be like

We all need role models to help us achieve the best of our talents. They show us how to be useful and how to link our passion to our activity. Here are a few of my many role models; I owe them everything:

•Hal Nutt, Purdue University; the first knowledgeable and uninhibited speaker I heard;

•James J. Rudisil, Civic Leader and Executive; the first person to tell me that he prayed for me daily;

•George Mowery, Shoe Salesman; the first Sunday School teacher who showed he cared in many ways;

•Willard Niesen, Watchmaker and Sunday School leader; he gave me my first class of boys to teach and great books to teach from;

•Will Rogers, Humorist; I admire his wisdom, humility, compassion, and generosity;

•Robert Hull, President, MONY; an industry leader who never hid his faith;

•Stan Hale, Vice President, MONY; he taught me it is all right to quit, but never to do it;

•R.J. LeTourneau, Businessman; he practiced reverse tithing. He kept 10 percent and gave 90 percent;

•Curtis Hutson, Editor and Pastor; his simplicity and boldness for the cause of Christ inspired me;

•Daws Troutman, Founder of Navigators; exceptional for his love for God's word and his encouragement for others to memorize it.

Speaking tool #10: Mentors—Someone to teach us

"The truly educated have been mentored, either in person or by reading or association, by superior minds with greater skills and mature spirits."—Fred Smith

Fred Smith gives credit to Maxey Jarman, his mentor, for much of his success. If you don't have a Maxey Jarman, you can still find more education that you need in books. This has been especially true in my life because all of my mentors have been in books. I've read many of my mentors several times and even memorized chapters. I could list at least 100 "book mentors," but here are the ones that helped me the most in my early years:

1. *Lectures To My Students*—Charles Spurgeon
2. *My Utmost For His Highest*—Oswald Chambers
3. *Perspectives*—Richard Halverson
4. *How I Raised Myself From Failure To Success In Selling*—Frank Bettger
5. *How To Turn Your Ability Into Cash*—Earl Prevette
6. *Reality Therapy*—Dr. William Glasser
7. *The Normal Christian Life*—Watchman Nee
8. *Prayer*—Hallesby
9. *What The Bible Is All About*—Henrietta Mears
10. *The Pursuit of God*—A.W. Tozer

You may have the complete list of my book mentors by calling 800-233-BOOK (2665).

Charles E. "Tremendous" Jones is president of Life Management Services, Inc. and Executive Books; serves on the advisory board of Investment Timing Service, and is chairman of Pneumedic Corporation. He was born in Alabama and grew up in Pennsylvania. He now resides in Mechanicsburg, Penn., with his wife, Gloria. They have six children and six grandchildren. For more than a quarter century, thousands of audiences in America, Canada, Mexico, Australia, New Zealand, Europe, and Asia have experienced non-stop laughter as "Mr.T" shares his ideas about life's most challenging situations in business and at home. He is the author and editor of eight books, including *Life Is Tremendous: 7 Laws of Leadership,* which has sold over one million copies.

The 12 Biggest Pitfalls To Avoid On The Road to Successful Speaking

14

Tom Winninger, CSP, CPAE
Winninger Institute
4510 West 77th Street, Suite 210
Minneapolis, MN 55435
612-896-1900
Fax 612-896-9784

Palms sweating? Breaking out in hives? Heart pounding? For many, giving a speech can result in these and other uncomfortable symptoms. It doesn't have to be that way.

My philosophy of successful speaking is the same as that for successful sailing. The winners are those who make the fewest errors. If you know about the most common pitfalls that trip up speakers, I'm guessing that you will avoid those errors and be more successful in your platform performances.

Following are 12 mistakes that often result in a truly lousy speech, each followed by suggestions of how you should do things right. In other words, not only am I willing to let you learn from my mistakes, I'm prepared to let you in on my secrets of success also. Here we go with the Don'ts, followed by the Do's:

1. Wing it. You're too busy to spend hours preparing for one speech, so just make it up as you go along. If you fumble, tell the audience about your hectic schedule. Besides, spontaneity makes for a good presentation.

Professional speakers know that the number one ingredient for successful speaking is preparation. The pros *never* wing it; they put hours—sometimes dozens of hours—into each speech, even if it is on a topic they have addressed many times. I don't know a single professional speaker who doesn't create an exhaustive outline for every speech; most follow that outline with a word-for-word written text that they then practice repeatedly, committing most of the script to memory.

If you want your audience to be able to understand and follow your thoughts, those thoughts should be presented in logical order. If your ideas aren't in order, it's difficult for the listener to connect the points you're trying to make.

Begin by making a list of things you want to share, then decide which one is the best to do first, second, and third. If you're talking about the history of the United States, for example, you wouldn't talk about the Civil War before Columbus discovers America.

Here's something I do when I'm ready to begin writing. At the top of each page, I identify my audience: what they do, why they're attending, etc. Then I keep my audience in mind and gear my remarks to them as I write the speech. I call a couple of people who will be in the audience to find out more about them, then I use them as examples during my presentation.

If you are called on to speak on a subject you know nothing about, learn to say no, rather than trying to wing it. Say, "I know quite a bit about that topic, but I don't believe my experiences will bring to the platform enough of what the audience needs. My expertise really lies in..." If you do this, often people will modify what they want.

If you're going to speak on a subject on a regular basis, read everything you can on it. Anticipate books to be published next year, then call the author and say you'd like to have a galley copy. Sometimes authors will send galley copies to people simply because they are always looking for people to endorse their material. We sent out about 400 galley copies of my last book. By getting galley copies of books, you get ahead of the subject matter that's in the market and become more of a futurist.

2. If you focus on just one topic, the audience might start to yawn. Better talk about a lot of different things, so the audience will think you're an expert in lots of areas.

Professional speakers know the importance of having a single focus. The best speakers don't try to accomplish everything; they convey one message, but they convey it more strongly and memorably than the audience has ever heard it conveyed before.

Before you speak—before you even begin writing your speech— determine your objective. Then focus on achieving that objective.

I relate most speakers to the Alice in Wonderland story where Alice is chasing the rabbit. She runs under a tree in which a Cheshire cat is sitting. Nearby is a signpost with 15 signs pointing in different directions.

"Which road should I take?" she asks the cat.

"Where do you want to go?" the cat responds.

"I don't know," Alice says.

"Well then, any road will take you to nowhere," the cat replies.

I think most presentations are a road to nowhere because speakers don't establish at the very beginning where they want to go. You must have that passion to follow a single focus or your net results will be lost.

3. If it's a good message, it'll work for everyone who hears it, so why worry about this particular audience? Give them the same speech, just throw in the manager's name a few times.

Every successful speaker knows that customizing each presentation to fit the audience is a great way to win the audience's attention and approval. People want to hear about things that are part of their business or personal life, as well as things that can help them be more successful in their careers. Give your audience ownership of your focus.

Participants will be more inclined to have ownership of your concepts when you use their terminology. The president of a company might give the same presentation to stockholders that he gives to his managers, but he tailors the presentation to the uniqueness of each group.

Customizing means you have to get to know the audience. If you are speaking at a meeting and haven't had time to do any preparation beforehand, wander around and work the crowd when you get there. Then you can draw people into your presentation and become integrated with the audience. What if you have people in the audience with a great variety of businesses and backgrounds? I call this the Heinz 57 group. I would pick out three focuses that everyone can relate to and go with those.

Customize the words you're saying to the group you're saying them to. You don't want to talk engineering concepts to a garden club. Use lingo pertinent to the audience; it enhances your credibility.

Also, be aware of how many times you say "I think" or "I say." Instead, talk about "you, your" and "we." This draws the audience to you, giving them the feeling you are part of the group.

Remember that what the audience needs and wants to hear is more important than what you want to say. Seek a group in search of a solution rather than a solution in search of a group. It's better to come to the platform knowing the group is seeking some kind of solution and adapt your solution to their need than it is to come to the platform, give them your solution, and let them try to figure out what the need is. Some novice speakers spend so much time on things that listeners aren't concerned with, and so little time on what the audience really cares about, that they lose all control. Professional speakers know better.

4. Don't practice your presentation aloud before you give it. You know what your voice sounds like, so why waste time listening to it?

A speech is verbal, so you need to hear it before you give it. When I first started speaking, I would get up early, go down to the meeting room, and actually do the entire presentation out loud, in the room, with the visuals, with a microphone. I recommend you do the same. If you don't have that luxury, use a tape recorder and practice it in your car.

One of the best things practice does is give you confidence, and that's very important for every speaker, non-professional and professional alike. You didn't think professional speakers had to worry about pre-speech jitters? Well, sometimes we do. Most people who look very confident come to the platform with some level of fear; they just know how to control it.

Art Linkletter and I did a rally in San Diego several years ago. We arrived at the airport at the same time, and he asked me if I wanted a ride to the hotel in his limousine. I was very new at speaking at the time and was scared to death to speak at this rally, which would have an audience of 12,000 people.

"Do you ever have fear?" I asked Art.

"Yes," he said. "Fear is part of being a speaker. I just have my butterflies flying in formation." The more organized you are, and the more you have practiced, the more you will control your fear.

Outline your presentation and work from key points. Know the first two to three minutes better than you know anything else in your presentation, because this is when you are most likely to feel nervous. Use support visuals; they will make you more comfortable. I occasionally do a presentation on telephone marketing and have a phone with me. I hold it in my hand and get comfort from it.

Even though I make more speeches every year than most people will make in a lifetime, I still get to the room early and check the overhead and the mechanicals to make sure everything is ready for my presentation. I cue the tape, line up the projector, and bring the controls to the platform. It's what every speaker should do, every time.

5. Practice just-in-time arrival. Sitting around waiting until it's your time to speak may make you nervous. Besides, someone else was in charge of getting the room, the microphone, and everything else ready for you, and you assume they did their job. Your only job is speaking.

Leaving preparations to someone else, and arriving just before you are scheduled to talk, are risky business. Do you like to gamble with your reputation?

Arriving "late" is arriving when 50 percent of the audience is in the room. Allow yourself time to get comfortable with the room and the people in it. Go up, turn on the mike, and count to 10. Or ask a volunteer to stand in the back of the room while you test the mike to make sure the sound is coming out loud and clear.

Have you ever been in a presentation when the speaker used graphics the audience in the back couldn't see? When you are invited to speak, ask how big the room is, then prepare your visuals accordingly. I was at a presentation recently where an accountant used visuals that could not be read from the back of the room. It was very disconcerting because 50 percent of his material involved those visuals.

6. Start with a joke. Sure, you can pull it off. They laugh at your jokes at the office, don't they?

Typically, amateurs get up and tell a joke because they think everyone does it. Professionals don't. They usually tell a personal story or a humorous illustration.

Most speakers aren't comfortable until eight minutes after they start their presentations. The more risks you take in the first eight minutes of a talk, the greater your chance of giving a lousy presentation. Use a joke when you're more relaxed and in control and can take more risks.

Instead of beginning with a joke, use what I call a "Grand Opening." Ask a question, give a quote, recite a rhyme or short poem, tell a personal experience.

I often begin by stating a promise: "The reason I came here today is to show you how to increase your sales by $10,000 in the next 26 days." It gets the audience's attention.

You can ask a question: "When was the last time you had... ?" Or tell a short story. But keep it short to be sure that the audience doesn't get caught up in the story rather than the principle. And, be sure you use your own stories. If you're going to speak on a regular basis, you need to collect stories or personal experiences you've had. If you're going to use a joke, pick one that so closely resembles an experience you've had or an attitude you have that it naturally becomes bonded to you.

Here's another winning tip: Use statistics. They draw attention to you or to the subject and overwhelm people who might be your aggressors. Ninety percent of the population will not question a statistic.

7. Apologize for not being a professional speaker, so the audience won't expect too much. Then, when your speech is good, they'll be surprised.

If you draw a conclusion about yourself at the very beginning of your presentation by saying you're not a very good speaker, you are already asking for forgiveness for giving a lousy speech. If I tell you, even before we start golfing, that I'm not a very good golfer, you're going to focus on the things I don't do well. It's the same with speaking.

Here I'll share a tip to help you get your speech off to a better start. Give the emcee or introducer some comments you would like her or him to make when you are brought up to the platform. I might ask her to say, "I've asked Tom to spend a few minutes sharing with us some things he's been researching that are critical to what we need to be doing to be successful." That's a nice little introduction that makes me feel confident and lets me know how I should phrase my first couple of sentences. And it's not uncommon to make such a request.

8. If the message you have to convey is good, it really won't matter how you present it. Just read the speech; don't throw in a lot of gestures or put a lot of emotion in your voice. And avoid looking at the audience too much—it makes you and them feel uneasy.

How you say something is often as important as what you are saying verbally. An effective speaker understands that his or her voice, body, gestures, movement on the platform, eye contact with the audience, and other aspects of delivery are critical elements in a presentation.

Stand up straight; don't lean on anything. When you use hand gestures, don't physically point at people but gesture *toward* them. All gestures should come from the center of your body and move away from you. Start at your chest and gesture outward.

Dress appropriately. A presentation, whether or not it's in a casual environment, should have some semblance of formalism to it. I do not put my hands in my pockets while I'm speaking. I wear blues rather than reds, yellows or grays, because research shows that blue tends to lead your audience to a more comfortable feeling about your subject.

Modulate the pace and style of your speaking to the importance of your point. Don't be afraid to raise your voice when you say something significant; nothing you can do will lose an audience's attention more quickly and surely than talking so softly they can't hear you.

I speed up immediately before I make a very important point, then slow down when I make the point. Recently, I had a graphic display on the side of the room. I moved very quickly to the display, stopped dead at the display, then slowly made my point. I got the audience's attention in the rush, then held their attention while I made the point.

Strive for an animated face; it captures people's attention. Raise your eyebrows, smile in the middle of a comfortable thought, make your face intense. We've all seen speakers stand up and talk about a subject that they felt passionately about, but they did not demonstrate that passion physically. It lessens the audience's interest in the subject.

If making eye contact makes you nervous, pretend you are standing before a room full of individuals. Speak to one person at a time, then move your eyes from face to face. This draws the audience in and personalizes your speech.

Never, *never* read an entire speech. Instead, write down the points you want to make and the illustrations or examples you will use to make your points. Commit those illustrations to memory; the rest will follow. Good speakers go to the platform knowing two things: the points they want to make, and what illustrations they are going to use to support those points.

9. Be slick. When you are up there in front of an audience, they are expecting a performance, so you'd better give them one. You're the star here, so act like a star.

The platform is like a TV camera; it doesn't lie. If you are going to stand on a platform in front of an audience and pretend you're slick, people will look for reasons to knock you down. Don't try to be something you are not. The audience sees through speakers who are fakes and doesn't accept as truth anything they say.

10. Run long.

This "don't" needs little explanation. The best way to impress an audience is to finish early. If it is obvious that you haven't finished making all your points, you can say, "Well, I didn't get it all done." The audience will forgive you. It's better to run short and get invited back.

11. You've run beyond the time limit, but you promised a question-and-answer period. So go ahead—keep them overtime. Whatever they had planned can wait.

Non-professional speakers do this all the time. They use all the scheduled time for their presentation, instead of allowing time for Q&A, which often proves to be as informative a part of the program as the speech itself.

Instead of making this common mistake, stop early. Say there are several other issues you could address, but you'd rather take questions from the audience.

Don't begin the Q&A session with, "Do you have any questions?" Instead, say, "What questions might you have?" If no one responds, have a couple of prepared questions. Once you stimulate the group by giving an example of the kind of question you are willing to take, you'll get questions.

When receiving a question, you can do one of four things: handle it, pass it off, pass it back, or delay it. You can handle it by answering the question. You can pass it off by saying, "We need to put a group together to discuss that more fully, because in the time we have left it would be impossible to address it effectively." You can pass it back by saying, "Jim, if I would have asked you that question, what would have been your response?" Or you can pass it back to the group by saying, "Does anyone have a response to Jim's question based on some of the things I've talked about so far?" You can delay it by saying, "That's a wonderful question, and I would like to spend a little time focusing on it before I give an answer. If you will meet me after the program is over, I will look forward to addressing it personally with you."

12. Don't spend a lot of time at the finish line. By the time you get to the end of the speech, everybody has heard all your ideas. Just make your final point and say good-night.

Many speakers tend to finish and die, like a balloon running out of air. Professional speakers, on the other hand, understand that the *end* of the speech is just as important as—if not *more* important than—the beginning. This is your opportunity to leave your audience with memorable thoughts, words, and images. Don't let the opportunity pass you by. Try to find a closing illustration that ties together everything you've said thus far.

Giving a speech doesn't have to be a traumatic event. Preparation is the key to good speaking. If you prepare, practice, personalize, and finish on time, you'll finish a winner.

As I say at the end of my presentation more than 100 times a year, "If you use what I've shared with you here, you truly will stand up, speak up, and be remembered. And in the long run, you will make a difference in the lives of other people."

Tom Winninger, referred to by his colleagues, clients, and friends as "America's Market Strategist," has a unique ability to work within industries to create strategies that gain market advantage. His market strategies have been featured on CNBC's First Business program, in *BoardRoom Reports, Venture*, and *Success* magazines, and published in over 30 other trade journals, magazines, and newspapers. He is author of the best-selling book *Price Wars: How to Win The Battle For Your Customers!* He is the founder of Winninger Institute for Market Strategy, a research institute creating marketing strategies for America's premium companies. His companies have received the Blue Chip Enterprise Award from the U.S. Chamber of Commerce for market resilience. Tom was a nominee for America's Entrepreneur of the Year Award. He holds the coveted CPAE (Council of Peers Award of Excellence) designation for his lecture skills.

The Architecture of Emphathy and Effectiveness: Building A Winning Presentation

15

Jim Tunney, Ed.D., CSP, CPAE
P.O. Box 1500
Carmel, CA 93921
408-649-3200
Fax 408-649-3210

Year after year, psychologists rank having to speak in front of others as the thing people fear the most. This fear crosses all educational levels and all personality types.

The college grad who was Big Man On Campus and the most socially engaging of his group can still be shy standing on the dais with the eyes of an audience staring at him. The CEO who manages million-dollar decisions without stress can become tongue-tied giving the keynote address at the annual shareholder's meeting. The expert who knows his research every which way to Sunday and operates an electron microscope with ease may blush and stammer when a microphone appears.

Being asked to speak indicates someone values your knowledge, opinions, or ability to inspire. Fear and self-consciousness are not good enough reasons to deny yourself the benefit of such recognition. Neither are they valid as reasons to shun opportunities to advance your career or make a difference in the lives of others. The fear and self-consciousness of speaking before others can be defeated by preparation, insight, and practice.

The following discussion will give you a plan, the architecture, for building a presentation that allows you and your audience to feel at ease. The steps outlined here will help you avoid the big gaffes and will assure that your audience hears your message, so that you and your audience have fun. That last—the bit about fun—is too often overlooked. It's a DO. Have fun.

Here we go.

Manage the internal energy

The rule of thumb is that an hour on stage requires the energy of a standard eight-hour working day.

We're human beings. We expend a tremendous amount of unconscious internal energy in the dynamics of self-consciousness. This is true even for pros who are outwardly calm, prepared, and practiced.

In the month, the week, the day, the hour before your presentation, plan for the energy demand. Physically and mentally train as an athlete. Be healthy, stay fit, and exercise, even on the road. Eat and sleep properly.

The physical aspects are the easier part. Also do the emotional work. Separate practice sessions with alternating quiet times. This will add confidence and help you peak, with maximum energy, at the right time.

Write your message fully, then simplify

While preparing your presentation, see the goal line. Know where you are going. You can't chart a course without a destination. Knowing what you want to accomplish (the close of your speech) will help you organize your points and set a pace that will work for your audience and the time allotted.

In football, we have the rule of four and ten. You have four downs to accomplish ten yards. Make those ten yards, and you are rewarded with four more downs.

The points you design in your presentation are like the plays on a scoring drive. Each point (play) must stand on its own, and then be followed by the next to form a series, a continuous push toward an exciting conclusion (the touchdown). To do this, write fully, then simplify.

Whether you are an outliner, a start-at-the-beginning-and-drive-to-the-end type, a keypointer, or you dictate and then edit, the same rules apply. Get it all down, then shape it for strength. Save the best of the culls for use in the longer version of the same message, but do not be afraid to toss the debris. Simplify and shorten toward strength, for impact.

Align yourself with your audience

Your message will be better received if your audience senses you as one of them. Picture yourself sitting in that audience, listening to the speaker, asking the WIIFM question, "What's in it for me?"

Any message, no matter how potentially powerful, useful, even mandatory, is undermined by psychological distance. The answers to WIIFM questions must be clear and personal to your audience. Convert "you" to "we," and be explicit early in your presentation on how your audience can relate your message to their business, family, and personal lives.

Quote frequently, credit always

OPEs—Other People's Experiences—are routinely one of the chief ways we learn in life. As that great American philosopher, Yogi Berra, said, "You can observe a lot just by watching."

What we learn from paying attention to other people's experiences becomes the backbone of our own choices and can be the spine of any speech. You can provide inspiration and add to your audience's own memories and experiences by sharing with them lessons from the lives of others. When I'm called upon to give a motivational speech, I take great pleasure in sharing the inspiring feats I've witnessed, whether by athletes at the Special Olympics or at the Super Bowl. I enjoy watching the audience smile and grow thoughtful as they integrate the story to their own situation.

Sharing and building bonds in this way is one of the great joys of speaking; however, when using OPEs, give credit. Even if the quote or story is in the public domain (the copyright has expired or there never was such protection), give credit. Indicate whose experience or words you are referring to. It is more effective (and simply honest) to credit your source than it is to omit credit, silently pretending it is original to you. Believe me, someone will know and that alone will undercut the effectiveness of your presentation.

Practice, aloud and with an "audience"

Practice, practice, practice. The reason you've heard it over and over and over is because it's true. Saying your speech aloud into a tape recorder and then listening critically one time is worth ten silent read-throughs.

In the same way, one stand-up practice in a mock setting with friends and family members as an audience is worth ten read-alouds. Preparation is more than fact-finding and effective writing. Gaining the more subtle skills—voice control and modulation, paper and equipment handling, posture and presentation, humor and timing, ease and confidence—requires preparation. Preparation includes practice, *real* practice. Heed the coach's maxim: Practice doesn't make perfect; *perfect practice* makes perfect.

Do an equipment check

Few things are as certain to break the rhythm, impact, and effectiveness of a presentation as an equipment snafu. An overhead projector that doesn't work or a microphone that goes out in the middle of your talk is not only embarrassing to you, it's irritating to your audience. The good news is that most equipment problems can be prevented.

Well in advance of the scheduled appearance time, *personally* check all audio-visual equipment. Give yourself enough time to solve a problem if there is one.

Start with sound. Listen to your voice over the audio system, and have others in the room move around the room to check all speakers and listen for "dead spots." Check the volume. Listen to the tone to hear if it is properly modulated. Test the feedback. Check the cords for distance and free movement. Have a back-up mike readily available.

Be just as specific about the components of every system you use—slide projector, pointer, audio or video playback, teleconferencing rigs, etc. Be thorough, and accept personal responsibility. You'll be dealing with, or rewarded by, the results of your forethought and action.

Enter ready

Anticipation and high energy are benchmarks for being ready. No matter how many times you've spoken before a crowd, that rush of energy will be there. Harness it and use it for your own benefit.

Remember to breathe, deeply. This is a full-day's-energy-in-an-hour event you are beginning. Temper the high energy and anticipation by focusing on your audience. Notice how they are hearing you and adjusting their attention and focus to you. The connection you make in your first three minutes will set the tone for how your audience responds to you, and therefore, to the message you have for them.

Provide your own introduction

Write an introduction that fits the occasion. Make it short, lively, directed to your audience, and include a clear pointer to the start of your presentation. Knowing what will be said just before your remarks begin will make you more relaxed and confident about your opening. In fact, consider your introduction as the opening to your program.

Have a typed, easily-readable copy of the introduction for your introducer. Review it together. Make sure the introducer knows how to pronounce your name correctly. Don't assume everything will go just as you imagine. Stand ready to improvise if need be. Have an ad-lib or two ready to bridge a possible awkwardness.

Don't apologize

How many times have you seen nervousness and self-consciousness cause a speaker to start with an apology or suggest that he or she is not worthy of making the presentation? Such an apology makes your audience squirm and, instead of breaking the ice (the intent), it creates doubt where there should be sure direction.

Part of the emotional work referred to above consists of programming your mind for success. Use quiet zones in your training and, in the minutes before you are introduced, to repeat affirmations that you are confident and competent, that you know your mission and your message, and that you will give an effective presentation. If, once you are on the dais, these visualizations fade and you hear "Unaccustomed as I am..." or some such hedge falling from your lips, stop. Say, "Whoops, that's another speech, from another time. Today, we're ..." and get right back on track.

Say thanks, by name

As a transition between the introduction and your message, recognize your introducer and the notables present (conference coordinators, CEOs, heads of states, etc.) who are known to your audience. This establishes a connection from the event to you and helps the audience see you as a part of their team and purpose.

Build on that sense of team and coordination by giving credit to the people responsible for bringing the event to the successful point of your presentation. Be sure that you know (and have rehearsed) the correct pronunciation of their names, as well as their titles and responsibilities in connection with the event. Do this without notes, if possible.

State that you are honored

Whether it is your one-hundredth speech for the local Rotary Club or your first corporate presentation, state simply and honestly your pleasure in being asked to speak. Describe something the group as a whole has recently accomplished, or single out one member for recognition. Honor your audience. Enter with a mindset of appreciation in yourself, and create that in your audience. Remember, this is an opportunity for you to help, to share information that many other people may never have.

Involve the audience at the outset

This might be as simple as asking them to give your introducer (use the name) a warm round of applause as thanks. Or, ask a question that calls for a show of hands. Audience interaction helps establish individual attention and communicates interest. They want to feel, and you want them to feel, that you are there for them and that you will be presenting issues important to them. Getting the audience on your team will give you confidence throughout the presentation.

Then, own the stage

Study the great performers. All the enduring entertainers—from Sinatra and Bennett to Midler and Streisand—command their territory. The stage is theirs when they are on it. They make you feel welcome to join them there. How do they do this? By loving what they do and having the courage to show that to you.

Show that you care

People don't care how much you know until they know how much you care. You can't get around this truth, nor its wisdom.

Go to your audience, physically and emotionally. It's best to touch their emotions before digging down into intellectual or

technical points. The rapport developed by sharing a story or incident of self-disclosure humanizes you, enlivens them, and sets
the stage for better acceptance of what follows. If it suits you,
leave the platform and go into the audience; physically join them.
Whatever your approach, develop empathy.

Speak clearly, with a varied pace and tone

There's no quicker way to lose an audience than to make them
struggle to understand you. Nervous energy is usually the culprit.

On one end of the spectrum, nervous energy can cause you to
spew too fast, eliding and overlapping words, causing a mumble-
jumble. At the other end of the spectrum, nervous energy can flat-
ten your tone, making you sound bored—or worse—like the syn-
thesized voice on the concourse train at the Atlanta airport: "The
train is leaving the station. Please move away from the doors."

Early in your presentation, establish a pace that you are comfortable with and that captures and retains your audience's attention. Watch your audience for cues. They will show—through
restless body language and the eye contact they stop giving
you—if you are losing them.

Use your eyes, as well as your voice

Looking directly into my eyes tells me you are addressing me.
Connect your message to your audience by seeing the individuals, eye-to-eye. A five- or six-second pause with your eyes (not
your voice) anchors that person to you. Think of it as a form of
persistence-of-vision, for you and especially for members of your
audience.

Treat your audience as one

Make eye contact with individuals; however, don't lose the
back of the room by playing only to those seated close to you.
Likewise, don't ignore those near you by looking over the heads
of the entire audience.

Think of the audience as your team—that while each member

is important, it is through their response as a whole that the strongest result will come. There is a distinct energy developed by any group of people, and no group develops quite the same kind or amount of energy. To develop the best rapport with an audience, see it as a live, singular entity.

Don't bellow

Your audience likes to feel they are having a conversation with you. Granted, your presentation is more monologue than dialogue. Still, your audience wants to feel their thoughts and private responses to your message are part of the conversation. They can't feel this way if you shout at them instead of talking *with* them.

There are times, of course, when strength of tone is a useful aspect of illustrating a story. Go ahead. Get loud, even yell, but *from* the story, not *at* your audience.

Don't preach

Leave the preaching to Reverend Billy Graham. He's the preacher. You're the speaker. The distinction is marked by two major features: your tone of voice and the verbs you use. Be careful of *should, must, always.* Just share—what you know, how you've learned it, and a willingness to admit mistakes. Let the audience know you are human, and looking forward *with* them, not *down on them.*

Don't cuss

There are too many ways to gain the warmth and attention of your entire audience without risking offense to even one. If you need to use "blue words," you haven't found the heart of your message.

Don't ramble

Rambling occurs in the absence of preparation. The rule for

concise writing applies here: The shorter the speech, the stricter the preparation. Digressions and roundabouts confuse, and lose, your audience. Keep sentences short, and headed where you intend.

Don't fidget

Playing with your clothes, shuffling your papers, tapping your fingers, fiddling with a paper clip or the microphone cord detracts from your message. A calm presence inspires confidence.

Don't be funny, be humorous

One time Charlie Jarvis was asked if humor was all that important. "Only if you want to get paid," he said.

Yes, you need humor. People want to have fun. Comics— Carson, Letterman, Miller—may make a point on the way to a laugh. Often as not, they use a simple juxtaposition of the odd with the ordinary to spring a response.

If you are on the dais as a speaker, not a comic, tie your humor to your message. As with the "Don't cuss" injunction above, avoid humor that denigrates people or conditions, that is sexist, or otherwise breaks the rule of a good-time-had-by-all.

Gizmos are great, but people are your purpose

It is easy to become entranced (or conned) and think that the latest is necessary. I admit a personal resistance to technology that pulls instead of pushes; still, even if you are eager for everything digitized, laserized, and new, don't hide the meat of your message with too much high-tech sauce.

Deal with audience distractions promptly and effectively

The cardinal rule is that if you had foreseen it, you would have prevented it. Once in a while, though, situations develop that pull the focus from you to the unexpected condition. Deal with distractions. Stop if you have to and enlist help, whether it is the on-site coordinator or a member of the audience to whom you can delegate an action that will solve the problem. Guide the assistance, and be specific and calm as you do so.

Pace the intensity

Audiences expect intensity. They like it. They arrive wanting an *experience*. They want the emotion, the meaning, the sense. To develop the flow and energy that delivers that to them, use variation in pace in the same way as a major league pitcher uses a change-up to keep the hitter concentrating. Monotones moan. Variety electrifies.

In music, it's the pause of silence between the notes that makes the melody. Include such pauses. They allow your audience to mentally massage and absorb your message. Use silence as a partner.

Close up, and with power

The question to answer is, "Will your audience leave the room better informed and stronger individuals because you were there?" When you can answer yes to this question, you will have rewarded your audience. You will have given them a gift.

Challenge your audience. Give them things to think about. Suggest specific can-do steps that will reinforce your message and make it meaningful.

End on time

Knowing how long pauses and laughter will add to the base time of your message comes from experience. Watch the time, as well as your pace and progress. It is better to close early than to run long. No matter how important your material, anything given beyond the time allotted may mean you will lose your hard-won audience.

Evaluate

As a part of your closing, encourage feedback from your

audience. Request comments. Provide a means for your audience to tell you what they liked and what you could have done that would have been better for them. Treat the evaluations—both your own honest assessment and the feedback that comes from your audience—as a part of the presentation, just as you consider the introduction the start. These are the book covers, and your message the book.

No one gives his or her best speech the first time, and no one ever becomes good enough to stop learning from each experience. This is true for everyone, including top professionals. Experience counts, *if* you learn from it.

Finally, express your appreciation

Write thank you notes and letters to those who helped make the event a success. Be direct and sincere. Remember, the opportunity to address an audience is a privilege for you, the chance to impart your technical knowledge or insights to others. It is altogether appropriate to express appreciation for this. Include a gift, if you like, especially one that is unique to you and appropriate to the occasion.

The professional way

Preparation, learning and mastering delivery skills, enjoying empathy with an audience—these are steps professionals use and which you can develop. As you do, the fear of speaking in front of others fades, and in its place comes enjoyment and benefit, for you and your audience.

Remember, have fun.

Jim Tunney, Ed.D., is first an educator (teacher, coach, principal, superintendent of schools, headmaster). Better known for his work as a referee in the National Football League, Jim retired from the field in 1991 after 31 years with the NFL, during which time he worked a record 29 post-season assignments, including 10 Championship games and three Super Bowls. His book, *Impartial Judgment—The "Dean of NFL Referees" Calls Pro Football as He Sees It*, was released in paperback in 1995. Always active in the community, Jim established the Jim Tunney Youth Foundation in 1993, to support community programs that work with youth to develop leadership, work skills, self-esteem, and wellness. As a professional speaker and as a past president of the National Speakers Association, Jim has earned the respect of his peers. He works most extensively in the areas of team building, leadership, motivation, customer service, and wellness.

You've Got To Be Lively or You'll Lose Them: Adding Vitality To Your Talk

16

Patricia Fripp, CSP, CPAE
A Speaker For All Reasons
527 Hugo Street
San Francisco, CA 94122
415-753-6556
800-634-3035
Fax 415-753-0914

Today's audiences are stimulation junkies. Their attention spans are about as long as that of a cucumber. The mere hint of boredom makes them start to fidget and go glassy-eyed on you. Their television-watching habits have coined a new term: channel surfing. With the advent of the remote control, no one needs to watch anything that stands still and begins to bore. Click, switch, fast forward, record, mute—all terms that show we can turn it off or tune it out when our boredom meter goes off.

Television and other media also mean audiences today are exposed to professional speakers and entertainers on a daily, even hourly, basis. When you speak to an audience now, you aren't competing with other business associates or even yesterday's general session speaker—you're being compared with the likes of Jay Leno, David Letterman and MTV.

While keeping audiences interested can be challenging, there are some techniques you can use that help retain your listener's attention. Most of these techniques are based on a simple principle: If you present an interesting message in an interesting manner, people will stay tuned.

Working with humor

A few years ago, I went along with a friend to a comedy workshop. I attended the workshop knowing that I am not as naturally funny as professional speakers such as Charlie Jarvis, CPAE, or Jeanne Robertson, CSP, CPAE. However, what I discovered at the workshop was that there are some basic principles about comedy that we can all learn and apply to our speeches and presentations.

One of the most valuable things I learned was to stop telling stories that "belonged to the world"—in other words, *other* people's stories—in favor of finding and building more humor within *my own* stories. It was a tough decision because a couple of the stories I was using at the time were tried and true openings for me. Nevertheless, I dropped them from my presentations because they were jokes rather than personal stories.

When Danny Cox, one of my fellow Speakers Roundtable members, decided to go professional some years ago, he went to the beach with a pad and pencil under his arm. Danny reviewed his life, identifying those experiences and situations that could serve as good—or bad—examples for other people. He wrote down the high points and low points, failures and successes. Then he turned his experiences into stories, and his failures and successes into lessons that enrich everyone who hears them. Danny uses some of these stories in almost every speech, varying them based on his audience, the focus of the speech, and the lessons he wants to teach.

Begin collecting your own stories. Include those sudden and stunning bits of insight that come to you as you're speeding on the highway. Or maybe you said something to a friend that was particularly funny or memorable. Write it all down. In other words, record your life as you live it. Doing this will enable you to tell original stories, rather than telling anecdotes that audiences have heard once too often.

Some time after attending my first comedy workshop, I went to a one-on-one session with the teacher of the workshop. I was president of the National Speakers Association (NSA) at the time, so when I brought my video for him to critique, I expected that he would not have much upon which to comment. Two hours later, we were still working on my opening story.

The teacher made me look at each character in the story. My thought had been that I was the narrator and I had to make that role lively, but that the other characters were secondary, so why agonize over them? The teacher's response was this: "You are only the narrator until you tell a story; then, you become every character in your story." I learned that by slightly changing my voice, my position on stage, my head movements and the like, I could make the characters come to life. Amazingly, the audience could now *see* my story as well as hear it.

Audiences don't remember what we say; they remember the pictures we create in their minds. The more we act them out, the more vibrant and alive each character or facet of the story becomes, the more the audience will remember them.

Another valuable lesson I learned from that first comedy workshop was how to "punch up" the important words in my talks. We all know that "punch words" or "punch lines" are the lifeblood of humor; however, we also need punch lines in our motivational or business programs. These are words and phrases that are critical to the point or laugh you're going for.

That first comedy coach taught me how to pick out the "punch words" in my talks and how to deliver them more effectively. For example, in one of my stories, I used to say, "I set a new goal that day."

"Patricia, the punch word is *goal*," my teacher said. So I changed the sentence to "That day I set a new goal." I rearranged the words so that "goal" would receive more emphasis. You're probably thinking, "Now, that's being picky!" But being picky about the details is essential to excellence in speaking.

Assume now that you are going to use the stories of your life—the ones you have collected by living—now and in every speech you present in the future. Spend time developing your stories; work on the wording and delivery so the stories have power and impact. Being meticulous about how you present your stories is vital to staying fresh and professional.

Working with the "I-You Principle"

This is an extremely important principle I learned from John Cantu, another comedy writing coach.

If a female comedian says "When I was a cheerleader...," she runs the risk that many of the women in her audience will look at her with resentment. They may be personalizing the remark, thinking such thoughts as, "My thighs were too fat to be a cheerleader" or "I was never pretty enough or popular enough or athletic enough to be a cheerleader." In short, the opening does not build rapport with an audience.

However, if the comedian says, "Have you ever had an experience so embarrassing that you wanted the ground to open up and swallow you?" Now, audience members begin nodding their heads. "Let me tell you about when I was a cheerleader.." is the follow-up line. In this approach, the opening directs the audience to look into themselves. It's something they can instantly relate to. Rapport is established. That's the "I-You Principle."

Here's another example. If you're talking about financial planning, you could say, "I always pay myself first—not the recommended 10 percent. I save 20 percent of my gross income." Audience members will probably start rolling their eyes or at the very least thinking to themselves, "Twenty percent?! Yeah right, then the mortgage company slaps a foreclosure on me."

Instead, you could say, "We're all hurting in this economy and saving money is more difficult now than ever. It's also more important than ever. So I say our goal is just saving money out of each paycheck. Sometimes it's 10 percent; maybe it's only one percent at other times. Making a habit of saving is the point." This puts the audience in your speech and instead of scoffing, they identify with what you are saying.

Look at your stories and consider how you can turn them around to put the audience's perspective into them. For instance, I used to say, "One morning I gave a speech for the IRS. After all, they get enough of *my* money, so I wanted some of theirs." Now I say, "One morning I gave a speech for the IRS. They get enough of *our* money, don't they?...so I wanted some of theirs." You'll be more effective at capturing and holding attention when you learn to draw your audience in. You don't want them to feel that your speech is something you are doing to them, but that you and your listeners are in this together.

Working with movement

Don't say verbally what you can say visually. This is a lesson I learned from watching the movies of Chuck Norris and Claude Van Damme. Norris said that his friend, the late Steve McQueen, advised him thusly: "Say the last word in the scene and don't say anything you don't have to."

I'm an enthusiastic and high-energy person by nature. I use a lot of gestures in personal conversations, and this trait carries over into my presentations. When I began working with a coach, he pointed out that I had a lot of repetition of movements. While presenting my material, he asked that I not use any gesture more than once. This was very difficult for me in the beginning, but I kept working at it because I learned the positive impact of having variety in your movements. A story that Larry Wilde shared with me illustrates this point.

At one of his comedy classes in Southern California, Larry asked his students to do their acts without using gestures. The first student began his act, but Larry stopped him. "Start again," he said, "but this time, don't use your hands." The student looked surprised. Even though the class joined Larry in telling the student that he was indeed using his hands, he wouldn't believe it. Finally, Larry asked him to do his act with his hands clasped behind his back. The student was so handicapped without his hand gestures that he could not remember any of his act.

The point is that while we may use gestures to go along with specific points or words in our stories, if we are not aware of our gestures, we can use them too often or too broadly. And while we may lose track of our gestures, the audience doesn't. Too many movements, particularly those you do unconsciously, can distract from your presentation. "Don't use gestures without complete control of them," Larry says. It's excellent advice.

A valuable tip I learned from speaking coach Ron Arden was that my gestures, facial expressions, and dramatic style in general had to be toned down when my talk is being projected on the big screen for the back of the room. Broad gestures and dramatic movements that look normal otherwise tend to lose sincerity simply by being viewed larger than life on the big screen.

In a talk I prepared for NSA, there's a part where I say "I love my life!" and simultaneously put my hands up and tilt my head back. I knew my image would be projected on the big screen, so I toned it down.

Another facet of movement is how much of the stage we work. I once asked a choreographer to watch a three-hour seminar I was doing and give me feedback from his choreographer's viewpoint. "You did a wonderful job at working the front of the stage on both sides, but you didn't do much with the depth of the stage," he told me. Now, I am more aware of how I stand on the stage. Depending on the material I'm using, I may stand half-way in the middle of the stage, deliver an opening line such as "The future belongs to those..." I pause, take two steps forward, then say: "...who create it!" It adds to the drama of the words.

A speaker's movements on the platform can greatly enhance the power of his or her words to create pictures in the minds of an audience.

Working with voice and speech

Our voices are truly vital to our presentations, and I've worked with voice and speech coaches specifically to improve how I use my voice. After my first consultation with Carol Fleming of The Sound of Your Voice, I was almost too nervous to open my mouth.

Carol explained that, as I have a British accent, I have good diction. However, I pronounce some words in such a way that they are not easily understood by the American ear. I worked with Carol for about six months to make audiences know that I was saying "hair" and "care" and not "hay" or "cay." I drilled on emphasizing my "r's."

Another important lesson I learned from Carol was to use short, simple declarative sentences and to cut out any useless words. "Imagine that each word you use costs you $10," a speaking coach once told me. "Which words are worth leaving in?" When I look at a story in my speech, I examine each word looking for emotion. Not each word is of equal importance, and you have to do the work for the audience by emphasizing those words that are necessary for understanding and are important to remember.

The power of the pause

One of the most effective techniques I learned from working with coaches is *not* using my voice. Pausing in exactly the right moment in your speech is often more effective than anything you could do with your voice or your body movements.

When Speakers Roundtable hired Ron Arden to work with us, one of the major things I learned was to pause more often. Professional speakers know their material so well that we have a tendency to talk too fast. We have to remember that our audiences haven't heard what we're saying; it's important to give them the opportunity to catch every word.

From Ron, I learned that the faster we speak, the more we have to open up our material with pauses. If we do not, we limit an audience's ability to absorb our stories and ideas. "It's amazing that most speakers think they get paid for sound, so they get very nervous if there is too much silence," Ron has said.

Using pauses and silences to punctuate your material will draw in your audience. Eye contact has impact, but you'll find that if, after making a point or delivering a punch line, you accentuate it by standing still and shifting only your eyes, the impact is much greater.

Vary your pace

Another key element in delivery is the use of energy levels. Studies have indicated that the beginning 30 seconds and final 30 seconds of a presentation have the strongest impact on an audience. These are the times when you should maximize the use of your energy.

Anyone who has heard me speak knows that I believe in coming out punching to grab my audience. But if you come out at absolutely your highest energy level, as you bring it down, your presentation is going to seem flatter to the audience. And if you stay at your highest energy level for the entire program, you run the risk of having your audience not believe in you.

As a high-energy speaker, I've had to learn to add more variety and pacing to my delivery. Many motivational speakers are wonderfully funny and have a high-energy delivery style, but if it is all the same level, it can come off as boring to the audience, especially with a long program. The secret of effectiveness is learning to use a variety of energy levels, so that your audiences will remain alert and interested in your material.

When I saw myself on video at an effective communications seminar a few years ago, I thought they were running the video on double time. The teacher said (and he was being kind), "Your strength is your energy, but you know with a symphony, it's soft and quiet and then it builds to a crescendo. The variety makes each element more effective." While you are on the stage, you want to stand, move, be serious, be funny, talk loud, talk softly—

in other words, vary your pace and energy level to keep your audience interested. As my friend Bob Murphey says, "Don't speak in black and white. Speak in technicolor."

The saving grace of "technique"

When professional speakers perform the same material time after time, it is sometimes difficult to make it look spontaneous and fresh. It takes high art and hard work. You have to know how to "search" for a word on stage and make your audience believe the word has escaped you for a moment. When there is a laugh or an emotional catch in your voice, you must make your audience *feel* it. "You don't have to speak from the heart every time you deliver the speech, but you have to create the *perception* that you are speaking from the heart," Ron Arden says.

Humor, movement, dramatic delivery, using your voice for maximum impact—these are all techniques that can be learned. I have studied these techniques diligently until they have become a part of not only my speech, but of me. It takes time and work, but it's worth it. Now I'm assured that when I arrive in potentially disastrous situations at an engagement—such as jet-lagged, stressed, sleepless, or coming down with the flu—I'll have techniques I can rely on, techniques that I can guarantee will help me deliver a top-notch performance.

Your audience will forgive you almost anything except being boring. That's why I work to change my talks from all angles—humor, words, movements, pauses. To be predictable would be boring. And the only kind of predictable any of us want to be is predictably good.

Patricia Fripp is a superb performer and an excellent example of a successful entrepreneur. An entertaining and inspiring speaker, she brings humor and perspective to life's day-to-day changes and challenges with practical and immediately-applicable techniques—techniques that have propelled her into prominence as a businessperson, author, and speaker. She holds the Council of Peers Award of Excellence (CPAE) and was the first woman president of the National Speakers Association. *Meeting and Conventions Magazine* named Fripp as one of the 10 most electrifying speakers in North America. She is author of the book *Get What You Want.*

A Speech Is A Journey 17

Art Holst, CPAE
Promotivation, Inc.
2001 W. Willow Knolls Road,
 Suite 206
Peoria, IL 61614
309-691-9339
800-238-9339
Fax 309-692-9559

Every speech is a journey—a journey for the audience and a journey for the speaker. For the audience, the journey may be headed in a specific direction, or it can be rather obscure and vague, with the eventual outcome uncertain. But for the speaker, the journey should always be well-defined.

The speaker should know in advance the roadway he or she expects to take, and where he or she wants to be when the journey ends. The speaker should be keenly aware of the material to be covered, time available for the "trip," and, most importantly, the vehicle he or she will use to escort the audience to its destination.

This chapter deals with what I feel is the most important part of this journey: the vehicle or combination of vehicles to be used along the way. A speech, like a trip, is best when it is exciting and interesting, as well as informative. And, in order for the trip to be all those things, it must be well-planned.

As a platform professional with more than 3,500 paid appearances, the vehicles I use to take my audience on our journey together are clean humor, football stories based on my 15 years as a National Football League official, and appropriate anecdotes from my life as a business and family man. I also use some poetry in my presentations. It is this combination of vehicles that I employ to take my audience along with me on a journey that will, I hope, lead my audience to a place of new understanding and inspiration.

Humor smooths the way

I come from Peoria, Illinois, the world headquarters of the Caterpillar Tractor Company. Caterpillar is the world leader in earth-moving equipment. They make bulldozers of all sizes, including back hoes for digging holes and ditches and many more pieces of big equipment designed to reshape the world. The specific piece of equipment I want to refer to here is the motor grader. This is the machine whose tires can tilt one way or the other and which has a blade to smooth a roadbed for a proposed highway or perhaps a building site.

"Well," you may ask, "what does this have to do with speaking?" My answer to you is this: To me, humor is the motor grader that smooths out the bumps and ruts of life and makes it liveable. God made us the only animal with the ability to laugh. He must have figured that if we couldn't laugh at some of our foibles, failures, and frustrations, we'd all end up in the loony bin!

Humor is a very delicate and serious thing. It can be, as my speaker colleague Dr. Charlie Jarvis so succinctly has defined it, "a painful thing told playfully." Witness the jokes or humorous stories we have heard told about death or illness. For example, this Henny Youngman line: "A doctor gave a man six months to live. He didn't pay his bill, so the doctor gave him another six months!"

I use the following story when talking about being able to laugh at yourself when things don't go as you planned. "Just to be nice, I sent flowers to a friend of mine who opened up a new branch of his business. I went out to congratulate him and, naturally, I looked for my flowers. What I found was a wreath with a bow on it that said, 'Rest in Peace.' I left in a huff, called the florist, and said, "I sent a guy flowers to wish him well in his new business and you sent him a wreath with a bow on it that says, 'Rest in Peace!'" The florist said, 'I'm not worried about you, Art. But someplace in this town, there's a guy being buried, and he's got a big bouquet of roses with a sash on it that says, 'Good luck in your new location!"

This story allows me to make a serious point. Sometimes our best intentions go down the drain. So, the selection of humor is not just a matter of whether or not it is funny; it is also a matter of whether it is relevant to the message.

In another example of the use of humor, I may be talking about why knowledge is so important for the sales or management person. I will use a comparison between NFL football and life.

When a football player comes to pre-season camp, he is expected to be in good physical condition. Before anything else happens, he receives a rigid physical examination. The number one priority in football, as it should be in any line of work, is to be physically capable to perform. After the physical exam, the player gets a playbook. That's the beginning of the knowledge factor. Complete knowledge of the plays and what the player is expected to do on each play is pre-supposed; the same as physical conditioning is pre-supposed.

I follow this information by saying something like this, "Knowledge isn't everything, but it is tremendously important." Then I tell how I was working a pre-season game in Memphis when a player cussed me. I whirled and yelled, "What did you call me?" He said, "Guess. You've guessed at everything else today!"

After that anecdote, I say to my audience; "You cannot guess; you've got to know. The key issue is, how do we use what we know to solve somebody else's or our own problems?" That little vignette is used to point out the relationship between knowledge and problem solving.

A smile from the start

Establishing the "humor vehicle" begins for me with my introduction. Our office sends the introduction, along with publicity materials, to the client prior to my speech. It is not a boring recitation of the circumstances of my birth, education, and whatever awards I may have received, deserved or not. My introduction is a short (45 seconds) and interesting "intro" which the chairman of the event gives, hopefully, as if it were of his own authorship. First, it puts the audience "in fun." I want the audience to subconsciously say, "Hey, this might be better than I thought! I might even wait to go to the restroom." Let me break down my introduction and tell you what each segment means in terms of the presentation.

"Our speaker today has been applauded by thousands and booed by millions." That's a mild, humorous put-down that always gets a little laugh from the audience. Remember, I want them to be "in fun." The introduction continues with these lines, "He has probably spoken in your city and, if not, he has surely flown over it." This establishes some immediate credibility. I want them to think, "This isn't the first time this bird has done this."

Next, the introduction says, "You see, he was a National Football League official, one of the most cursed, yet anonymous, men in the world." This line establishes general background information and also a little fun as it refers back to the "booed by millions" line. Then this: "Contrary to popular belief, he is quite normal in other respects." If the introducer emphasizes the word "normal," it will get a nice laugh.

This is a transition line to lead into the business side of my persona. The next line is, "He is president of his own company and crisscrosses the United States numerous times each year speaking for sales, management, marketing, and association groups of all kinds." Credibility is now being established in the business area. The audience should be thinking, "He is more than just a jock."

To continue: "This 12-months-a-year businessman and platform personality spent 15 years on the field as an official in the National Football League. He was a line judge who wore number 33 on the back of his striped shirt. He officiated four Championship games and Super Bowls VI and XII, and he is still at it, as he is now in the press box each weekend rating his fellow officials." Now the audience knows enough to feel I'm qualified and that I'm still active and not a total has-been. But, have they forgotten to be "in fun"? We take no chances by ending with these words, "Not bad for a man over 65 who wears glasses—as you might expect—and shows up with a limp! Let's give a warm welcome to Art Holst!"

Humor? A little. Credentials? Enough. Anecdotal set-up? You bet!! Now we are ready for one of the most critical questions. You have them in your vehicle. How are you going to lock them in—hook 'em—so that they are eager for the trip?

Following the introduction

The speaker's first minute is critical. I might respond this way, "Thank you, Mr. Schnubenstuben. That's the kind of an introduction that put George Bush where he is today (laugh). You had to bring up my age too—thanks a lot. I *am* past 65, and I see some of you fellas are getting close. Now that I've passed that milestone in my life, my whole life is upside down. When I sit down to eat at night, I feel sexy. When I go to bed, I feel hungry!" Do you see how the introduction set up my opening humor? My audience now knows that our time together is going to be fun. And, that response takes about 30 seconds, including laughter.

I also use part of the humor in the opening seven or eight minutes to poke fun at myself. No one is impressed by a speaker who is pompous and paints a self-important picture of himself or herself from the platform.

For example, I say this: "I came into the NFL in 1964, and that first year I was working a game in Cleveland. Cleveland's fullback was Jim Brown, a great football player. In that game, the Cleveland Browns were playing the Dallas Cowboys. Brown came through the line with the ball, and the middle linebacker for Dallas tried to tackle Brown. When he did, he grabbed Brown's face mask. I threw the flag, stopped the clock, and told the referee, 'I've got number 55 on the defense pulling the face mask. Personal foul. 15 yards.' At about that time, the middle linebacker jumped up, all six-foot-five, 255 pounds of him. He yelled, 'What did you call, dummy?' I said, 'Get back in there and play football before I bite your head off.' He said, 'If you do, you'll have more brains in your stomach than you have in your head!'" He was probably right. Regardless, the story is a crowd pleaser and takes some of the glow off my halo.

The humor in the body of a talk should help make a point, be told well, and should, of course, be clean. An occasional "damn" to make a point may be acceptable but, if there is any doubt, don't use it.

Some humor guidelines

Now I would like to share with you my "Lucky 13" humor guidelines:

1. Look for stories that fit into the message you want to get across.

2. Never say, "I'm going to tell you a joke...", or "I heard this one..." The humor should flow nicely through the speech.

3. Repeat all dialogue and become an actor or actress when telling a story or anecdote. For example, I might say, "I was talking before the Kansas Bankers Association, and I asked a young banker, 'How long have you worked at the bank?' He answered, 'Ever since the day they threatened to fire me!'" I actually become the young banker while I'm delivering that line.

4. Try to find multiple-laugh stories. Or, better yet, tell your stories with the right pauses or facial expressions to create extra laughs.

5. If you string some humorous lines together, use the "topper line" last.

6. Remember, the best humor is usually not a joke. It is about a thing or event *told* funny. Witness the success of comedians like Bill Cosby, Red Skelton, Jonathan Winters, "Flip" Wilson, and many others.

7. Train yourself to "think funny." Everything in life is funny, even illness and death, because humor can be a painful story told playfully. Here are a couple of examples:

• The patient asked the doctor, "How do I stand, Doc?" Said the Doc, "That's what puzzles me."

• A son sat by his elderly father's bedside in the hospital. Equipment was everywhere. Suddenly the old man started to gasp, turned grey, and said something in a very weak voice. The son leaned close to his father and said, "What did you say, Dad? Do you have some advice for me?" Very weakly, the old man gasped, "Yes! Get your foot off my oxygen hose!"

8. Look for stories in which the last word makes the story funny. If you can't find one with the last word funny, make it the last phrase or sentence. The words "oxygen hose" make the last story funny.

9. If a story doesn't get a laugh, or the laugh is not as strong as you think it ought to be, just go on. *Do not apologize or make excuses!*

10. Be "audience aware." See what works and what doesn't, and make notes afterward to ensure a better presentation next time. Remember, only an average person is always at his best.

11. Be courteous to your audience. Use stories and anecdotes that everyone can enjoy. I use some football humor, but I try not to overdo it because there are many people who don't watch or understand football.

12. Don't go too fast. This is an important detail that I, personally, have to be careful about. Emphasize key words or lines,

and don't step on your laughs. Let the audience enjoy this piece of the trip fully.

13. And finally—Be yourself. If you like to laugh with an audience, do it! If you are more comfortable with a dead-pan expression, fine! Whatever works for you is best. God made us all different from one another.

Learn from others, but don't copy. Don't be like the boy in school who scored nine out of ten on his test but flunked anyway. The kid at the desk next to him got nine out of ten answers correct and received an 'A' for his efforts. The boy who flunked said to his teacher, "How come I got an 'F' and Harry got an 'A' when we both got 9 out of 10 answers right?" The teacher said, "Well, Harry had the first nine right, as you did, and for his tenth answer he wrote, 'I don't know.' You, on the other hand, wrote, 'I don't know either.'"

Make it personal

Anecdotes are events from your life that are unique to your experiences and will help you to make your point in the telling of them. Whatever your background, whatever your lot in life happens to be, things happen to you that will interest others if they are told sincerely and well.

I have told this little anecdote a number of times when making a point on communications. "If you *can* be misunderstood, you *will* be," I say. I continue, "Jeff, the oldest of my four children, would get in bed at night and, if I was home, I would come into his room, kiss him goodnight, and say the Lord's Prayer. Finally, one night I said, 'Jeff, why don't you say the Lord's Prayer for us tonight?' He nodded and did a perfect job until he said, 'Lead us not into temptation and deliver us from the eagles!'"

"Obviously," I say, "the message given was not the message received. But, it must have worked, because we have never been troubled by the eagles since!" It is a true story, and one I shall always treasure.

I also like to tell the story about when I was a new official, and one of the coaches got upset at a call I made. He hollered, "What's your name, rookie?" I said, "Holst!" He said, "How do you spell it?" I said, "H-O-L-S-T." He said, "Just as I thought—no I's!" (No eyes—get it?)

I have a steel hip with a Teflon socket; I'm a bionic man, of sorts. I don't leap over buildings at a single bound—it takes three or four for the bigger buildings. I tell about getting hit by a huge tackle from the Buffalo Bills that finished off my hip. I don't have the time and space to tell the anecdote here as I tell it when I speak but, believe me, it is funny! Was it funny at the time? Certainly not! But is it funny now? I answer with a resounding "Yes!"

You ask why. It is funny now because humor can be tragedy separated by time and space and, as I mentioned previously in this chapter, humor is often a painful thing told playfully. Believe me, the event that sparked this anecdote was painful. It was a tragedy. The surgery ended my career a couple of years early. But only in my eyes was it a tragedy. Some of the coaches and players probably viewed it more positively.

One more parenthetical thought. Remember the introduction? The last line ends, "...and shows up with a limp!" It's a set-up line for one of the funniest anecdotes I use.

You can use other people's anecdotes but, if you do, tell your audience to whom the incident happened and when it happened. This adds to your credibility. Don't use another speaker's anecdote if there is a chance that he or she will be there or has been there recently. It hurts everyone. I was to follow a speaker several years ago and happened to arrive early enough to hear him speak. He used two or three of *my* anecdotes as his own. Luckily I was there, heard it, and readjusted my material. By the way, he didn't tell them very well either!

Keep track of the things that happen to you and ask yourself, "Will this piece of my life be interesting or funny or of help to others?" If the answer is yes, then use it.

Poetry that creates memories

One of the very best ways to get a point across to your audience and have it linger in their memories is to use poetry. However, poetry must be used correctly or not be used at all. Here are some guidelines:

1. Select the poetry you will use carefully so it is to the point.

2. Be sure the poem is not too long. Two minutes is the absolute maximum, and you had better do it well! I use the well-known "Touch of the Master's Hand," and it takes one minute and fifty seconds to do it right.

3. Never, never, *never* read a poem. Use poetry that you know so well you can give it anytime, anywhere, and without any doubt of your ability to deliver it well.

4. Slow down! Most speakers do poetry too fast.

5. Emphasize not only words, but pauses too. Emphasize not only loudness, but also quiet and softness.

6. Pause at the end, then drive home your point.

I want to close this chapter with a poem I use often that relates directly to the fundamental message of this book written by my colleagues and myself. Our hope is that you, the reader, will see us for what we really are—a group of men and women of varied backgrounds and talents trying in our own way to share our successes and failures from the platform, not just to earn a living but to help others and ourselves make a more meaningful life as children of our Creator. This is the real journey we are taking with you in this book because, you see,

> "I'd rather see a sermon than hear one any day.
> I'd rather one should walk with me than merely show the
>   way.
> The eye's a better pupil and more willing than the ear.
> Fine counsel is important, but example's always clear.
> The best of all the preachers are the men who live their
>   creeds,

For to see the good in action is what everybody needs.
I can soon learn how to do it if you'll let me see it done.
I can watch your hands in action though your tongue too fast
   may run.
And the lectures you deliver may be very wise and true,
But I'd rather learn my lesson by observing what you do.
For I may misunderstand you and the fine advice you give,
But there's no misunderstanding how you act and how you
   live."

Art Holst holds a bachelor of arts degree from Knox College, did graduate work at the University of Illinois, and served as a Captain in World War II. He has been a successful salesman and businessman, the administrator of Forest Park Foundation, a member of his local Chamber of Commerce, and a Rotarian. Art was a National Football League official for 15 years, officiating four Championship games and two Super Bowls. He remains active in the NFL today, observing and rating NFL officials and scouting college officials. Art has spoken before more than 3,500 audiences. His messages, custom-tailored to each audience, are drawn from personal experiences during his long career in business, sports, and civic affairs. Some topics covered are handling change, problem solving, discipline, teamwork, and how to laugh at yourself.

Danny Cox, CSP, CPAE
17381 Bonner Drive
Tustin, CA 92680
714-838-3030
Fax 714-838-1869

Murphy's Law—the philosophy that if anything can go wrong, it will—is a philosophy for pessimists, in my opinion. As an optimist, I tend to believe not only that things usually go right but that we can very often *make* them go right through our own efforts. This certainly applies to public speaking.

It's true that much can go wrong while you are delivering a speech or presentation, but many of the perils of the platform can be avoided. Believe it or not, it is the perils you will face when speaking that will have the most positive and long-lasting effect on your speaking expertise.

Paying my dues

Before I begin telling you what I've learned as a professional speaker, I'd like to tell you a little about my background. The expertise I accumulated before I began my speaking career had a lot to do with how and why I began speaking.

I was born and raised in the coal mining community of Marion, Illinois, and I graduated from nearby Southern Illinois University. I joined the military and became a pilot in the United States Air Force, flying supersonic fighters. In addition to being a test pilot, I spent a great deal of my time as an air show pilot. Those were the days when pioneers of jet technology had "the right stuff," and it was a pretty exciting experience for the son of a coal miner from southern Illinois.

One of the unusual tasks I volunteered for while in the Air Force was speaking to civilian audiences about the positive attributes of sonic booms. At the time, sonic booms were a fairly new phenomenon and, as you can imagine, there were some folks who weren't very happy with me or the Air Force. Since I was up there on a regular basis causing all that noise, I thought it would be appropriate for me to explain away the fears and objections civilians were encountering. I soon became known as the "Sonic Boom Salesman," thanks to my efforts to overcome people's objections to my work. I learned a lot about being persuasive when I was facing *those* audiences!

Later, when I returned to civilian life, I became a salesman once again. I joined one of the largest sales firms in the United States, becoming a branch manager in one short, challenging, and rewarding year. Thanks to a great team effort, we were able to double, triple, then quadruple all previous performance records. Those were the years when I learned and practiced the management style and people-building techniques that I now share with others in my speaking engagements.

Perils enhance performance

I learned during my years piloting a sales team, as well as during my years as a test pilot, that the things that go wrong—the things that challenge us—can be the impetus that brings out the best in us.

I've said "The Test Pilot's Prayer" on many occasions as I faced a major emergency at 40,000 or 50,000 or 60,000 feet. Out of necessity, the prayer is quite short:

Dear God, get this thing back on the ground and I'll taxi it in for you. Amen.

It would be hard to calculate how many times I've stood on a speaker's platform and felt the same sense of imminent disaster. It's safe to say it's been more often than I would like to admit. What got me out of those tough spots was having a lot of preparation behind me to back me up.

My definition of an excellent leader is one who anticipates problems and gets ready for them. That's what we need to do if we want to achieve excellence in speaking.

Fred Allen once said, "There's no such thing as an ad-lib." He was a professional, but the same goes for the non-professional facing an audience on the speaker's platform. Anything you can image (and some things you can't) will happen at one time or another. The good speaker will be prepared and be able to make it look like an ad-lib. Spontaneity, it has been said, is the ability to have many well-rehearsed alternatives. And that's what this chapter is all about: how to plan for the unexpected.

There are three basic components to handling potential perils of the platform: pre-program planning, room preparation, and the presentation itself. Let's start with pre-program planning.

A contact sheet works

I approach speaking as I used to approach air shows. Back then, people often said I was crazy for doing the things I did. What they didn't realize was how carefully planned every maneuver was. One word I never wanted to utter during an air show was "Oops."

In southern Illinois where I grew up, we had a saying that went, "It's OK to have a tiger by the tail...if you know what to do next!" Or, as that great 20th century philosopher, Evel Knievel, once said regarding his spectacularly-dangerous stunts that only lasted seconds: "You've got all that time up in the air to think about what it's going to be like to come up two miles-per-hour short at the other end." Yes, planning is important.

My best suggestion for heading off problems up front is to maintain a "contact sheet." My contact sheets help me to know everything possible about the company I'm going to be speaking for, who to contact (including a back up contact with home phone numbers), etc. (See Figure 1).

Figure 1 (front)

CLIENT INFORMATION

Engagement # _____   Level   1   2   3

Today's Date _____ Confirmation Date _____   Alphabetical File _____

Organization _____

Name/Title _____ Office # _____/_____

Assistant _____ Phone # _____/_____ Fax # _____/_____

Company _____ Home # _____/_____

Address _____

Meeting Location _____ City/State _____

Meeting Dates _____ Hold Dates _____ Confirmed [   ]

Type/Length of Program (s) _____

Start/Finish _____ Theme _____ Audience Size _____

Related Information _____

                              Booker _____ _____% Phone # _____/_____

Fee _____ Agency _____ Fax # _____/_____

Speaker at Previous Meeting (s) _____

Client Source _____ Phone # _____/_____

Back up Contact:

        Name _____ Position _____

        Address _____ Phone # _____/_____

Nearest Airport _____ Dist. to Site _____ Hotel Res. _____

Hotel _____

Met by: _____ Bus. Ph. # _____/_____ Home Ph. # _____/_____

Pick up by: ( ) Taxi   ( ) Rental Car   ( ) Hotel Limo   ( ) Priv. Limo   ( ) Other

Program Check List

Sent to Client	Requested From Client	Date Rec'd
____ Program Info.	____ Signed Contract	_____
____ Contract	____ Deposit of $ ____	_____
____ Photo	____ Hotel Confirmation	_____
____ Bio	____ Mtg. Brochure/Map	_____
____ Preview tape ____ Video ____ Audio	____ Mtg. Agenda	_____
____ AV/Set up	____ Trade Pub./Bkg.	_____
____ Handout for Dup.	____ Pre-Program Ques	_____
____ Pre-Program Ques.	____ Fee/Reim.	_____
____ Final Chklst.	____ Letter of Rec.	_____
____ Intro.	____ Final Checklist	_____
____ Invoice	____ Feedback	
____ TU Note		

Figure 1 (back)

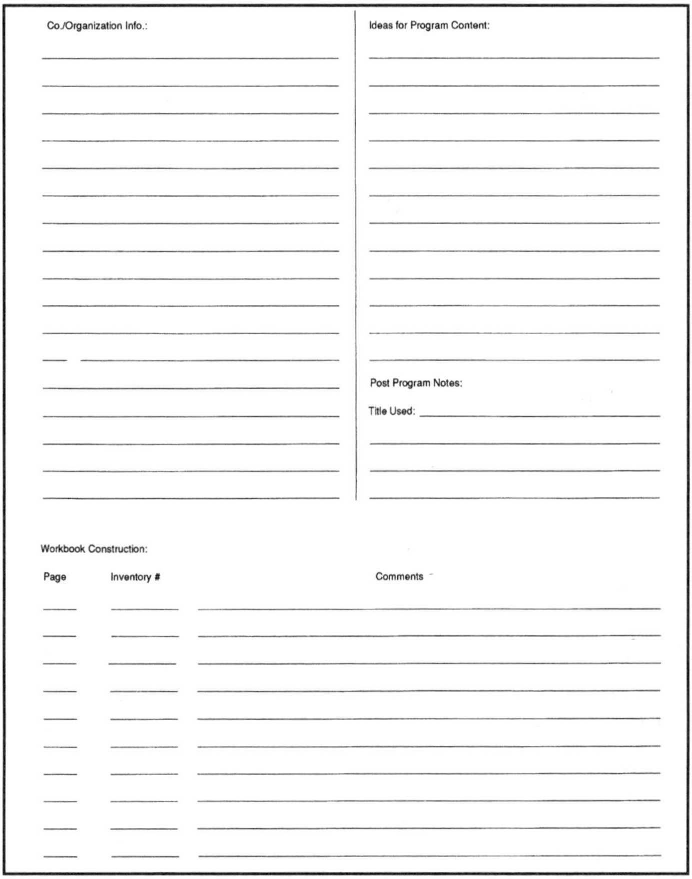

Co./Organization Info.:

Ideas for Program Content:

Post Program Notes:

Title Used: _____

Workbook Construction:

Page	Inventory #	Comments

You'll note that on the back side of my contact sheet, I go over with my client exactly what I'll be covering in my presentation, so that when I'm invited back, I won't cover the same ground again. Even though I don't tell jokes, I don't want to tell my true-but-humorous stories to the same audience twice. That half-chuckle/half-murmur audiences emit when they have heard a joke before will send chills up a speaker's spine.

The more I can know about the meeting at which I am speaking, the better prepared I will be. I send a pre-program questionnaire to gather information such as:

• What's the theme of the meeting?

• What does the organization do?

• What are the occupations of those attending?

• What are the significant advances in your industry in the past 18 months?

• On a scale of one to 10 (10 being best), how do you rate the average person in your audience in terms of customer service, energy, working priorities, innovation, commitment to the job, creativity, goal orientation, enthusiasm, problem-solving, and personal growth over the past 12 months?

• What are the most important things I need to know about your group before speaking to them?

• What are your expectations for my presentation?

• Is there anything new about this meeting vs. other meetings?

• What are some of the "buzz words" and their meanings that the audience relates to?

• Who are the top people (and their titles) from your organization who will be attending the meeting?

• Who else is speaking at this meeting, and what are their topics?

• What's happening immediately before and after my presentation?

• Are there any other questions I should have asked?

Room preparation

I send my clients a room diagram of exactly the way I want the room arranged when I speak (See Figure 2). It's helpful to my clients as well as to me to have the tables, chairs, and other items positioned properly for the best possible presentation. I want to walk into a room and feel it's *my room*, not someone else's. I even angle the chairs and tables, chevron style, because it breaks up the straight lines in most seminar rooms, making the environment warmer and cozier.

Room preparation goes beyond just sending a diagram. You've got to go in and physically scout your location. I go in the

Figure 2

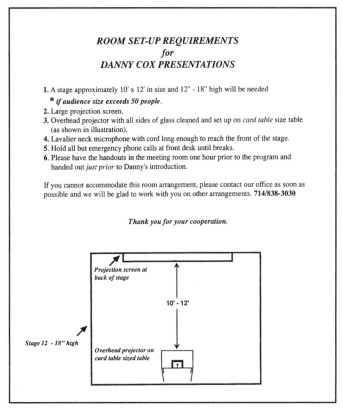

evening before, and the first thing I check is sound. Is there a meeting scheduled in the room next door while I'm speaking? Will their sound leak into my presentation? I want to know in advance if I need to make other arrangements. I check the room again the next morning at least an hour before the meeting starts to make sure the room hasn't been re-set for some reason after I've personally supervised the set up to my specifications.

Common complaints

Poor sound proofing and cramped space are two of the most common complaints about public meeting rooms where you'll be called upon to speak. For example, I like to see at least three feet between rows of chairs or tables. When the audience is more comfortable, you'll be more comfortable as a speaker and less likely to experience perils.

One of the first things I find out when I arrive at a speaking location is who will be in charge of the room I'm speaking in and what time that person is arriving. I've been speaking professionally for more than 17 years, and I've learned that you can't assume you'll be able to find the person in charge of the room when you need to. So I make it my business to hunt that person down in advance, introduce myself, and know where he or she can be located.

In the early morning, I conduct my S.A.L.T. check:

• Seating
• Audio-visual
• Lighting
• Temperature

If I'm the first speaker on the program, I want to be in the room before even the earliest early-bird in order to be sure things are right. When all eyes and ears are on you, your complete focus should be on your presentation, not on stage management. If the seating is wrong, it might take a few minutes to rearrange things. It's easier if people haven't already begun taking their seats.

Checking audio means finding out if the microphone is working, if it's in the right location, if the volume is correct and, again, knowing who to contact for adjustments. If there's going to be a meeting making noise next door, can the noise and distraction be reduced? If they plan to show a movie, the soundtrack can be loud and disruptive. Can one of the meetings be moved?

Checking lighting means not only making sure the lights are working in the room and in your speaking area, but also if the overhead projector or other audio-visual equipment is working correctly. These are all little things that can add up to big problems if you don't spend a few minutes checking them out in advance.

Temperature has a great deal to do with your audience's comfort level. When I'm prepping the room, I turn the heat up until I can feel it and then switch over to the air conditioning to see how long it takes to cool the room back down to a comfortable level. A room filled with people will heat up quickly and cool down slowly. If there are no ventilation or temperature controls in the room, know who you can contact to get the temperature adjusted quickly if the need arises.

Beware rooms with a view

If the room where you will be speaking has a view—particularly of a scenic panorama, the swimming pool, or a golf course—you don't want the room set up so that the audience is facing the distraction. The best position is with the audience looking directly away from the scenery. If anyone should be facing an attractive distraction, it should be the speaker. The best possible solution is to block off the scenery from everyone so that eyes and thoughts stay on your presentation.

Pay attention to where the coffee is set up. If it's in the front of the room near your speaking position, you've got a problem. Make sure the coffee is set up in the back. Are there elevators nearby? Will you be hearing the constant ringing of the elevator bells throughout your presentation? Make sure someone is assigned to keep the meeting room doors closed to minimize outside distractions, even if it's an attendee who does the monitoring for you.

Just before it's time for me to make my presentation, I brief the Master of Ceremonies. I always have a second copy of my prepared introduction, and I instruct the M.C. to read it *as written.* No paraphrasing or editing, I insist. If there is a hard-to-read word or phrase, point it out to the M.C. before he or she stumbles and embarrasses you both.

Some of these details may seem minor to you, but I wouldn't mention them if they hadn't caused me problems at some point or another. Just when you need to focus on your presentation, some small detail may erupt and distract you or your audience. Attending to small details can make a big difference in your success on the platform.

The presentation

The following are some simple and concise but important details to remember when you are planning the presentation itself.

• *Value the audience's time.* Keep acknowledgements to a minimum. Don't go on and on thanking people. The audience doesn't want to hear all that. Make sure the audience sees you take your watch off and lay it out where you can see it. The audience appreciates your letting them know how much you value their time.

• *Grab them.* Make sure that you begin with a grabber. The first words out of your mouth need to get their attention. Keeping a crowd's concentration is hard enough; you need to give yourself every advantage by getting them tuned into you right from the start. One of the best ways I've discovered to get the audience with you is to begin with a personal story that shows how you dealt with, and overcame, adversity or failure.

Every presentation I do begins with the story of how I personally destroyed a prestigious sales office. It's a true story. My first real management assignment after leaving the Air Force was such a total failure that I took the Number One office in my company's 36-office region and dropped it to last place, all in three month's time.

I tell my audiences how my boss came out to my office to personally tell me that he was already looking for my replacement. That was not only the shortest, but also the finest, motivational seminar I have ever attended. As it turned out, I got my act back together, didn't lose my job, and went on to lead my office to the record-breaking performance I described earlier. My point is this: Audiences can't believe that someone would stand in front of them and confess to such disastrous behavior. It gets their attention!

By contrast, if I were to begin my speech by telling the audience I've got all the answers and all they need to do is pay attention, they will not be nearly as inclined to listen. Getting the audience involved with the story you have to tell will make all the difference if they have to hear you speak for the next few minutes or hours or all day. Letting folks know that you are human and vulnerable to mistakes, just as they are, forges a good bond right from the beginning.

• *Use your own voice.* Believe it or not, it's possible to "learn a voice." Many people don't use their own voice when speaking in public, probably out of either an unconscious attempt to mimic a great-sounding voice they have heard, or from a self-conscious feeling about their own voice. It's important to be conscious of your own voice and to use it to the best of your ability. For one thing, mimicking another voice will lead to vocal fatigue and hoarseness more quickly than using your own voice.

• *Don't drink the water.* I was surprised the first time someone coached me not to drink water while I was speaking. A pitcher of water on a lectern is one of the most common sights in America. But drinking water on the podium distracts the audience, and it creates the sensation in your throat that it needs more moisture. Your vocal cords begin to tighten. If I drink water during a speech, my voice begins to squeak so loud the audience can hear it. That's another reason to avoid water.

One of the best things you can do during a break or while the audience is laughing is to blow against your throat. Exhale in a panting sort of way in order to expand the muscles inside your throat and lower your voice back to its normal range. You will hear your voice get lower and more comfortable.

• *Learn to control the audience.* Maintain eye contact with the audience throughout your presentation. And don't forget the eyes in the back of the room. It's a natural tendency to work the folks in the front few rows; the best speakers never forget to include *everyone* in the room.

To help hold the audience's attention, try asking rhetorical questions. Salt your speech with questions such as, "Have you ever wondered why...?" or "Has this ever happened to you?" These types of questions help the audience personalize what you are talking about and put themselves in the picture. If they have drifted away, questions bring them back. Another technique is to thump the lectern a couple of times. That usually gets the group's attention.

Recently I saw a piano player in a cocktail lounge control a crowd more effectively than I've ever seen it done before. Here's how she did it. She would look at every person and, when they made eye contact, she smiled at them and moved on to the next person. Her simple-but-effective technique locked everybody in.

The reason I stress keeping your audience's attention is to keep them *with you*. When an audience is with you, they will be much more forgiving of the perils you might encounter. When the audience is concentrating on what you are saying, they tend to ignore distractions.

One of the most effective tools in your speaking arsenal is a *pause*. Pausing gives you, the speaker, an opportunity to collect your thoughts, and it gives your audience a chance to soak up your words. Most of all, the pause is a tool you can use to regulate the pace of your delivery and maintain control.

When I first began speaking, I had a tendency to rush. I felt there was too much information and too little time. What I was giving up in my hurried delivery was the opportunity for *emphasis*.

It's natural to let yourself run on when you are talking about something very familiar to you. However, you need to concentrate on the material you are delivering to make it meaningful to your audience. Pausing now and then for emphasis slows you down and paces your delivery. The audience won't concentrate on your material any more than you do.

When I was learning to fly in formation in the Air Force, one of the students in my class asked the instructor what would happen if the lead airplane led the other airplanes in the formation into the side of the mountain. The unflappable instructor, who had been emphasizing the importance of following the lead airplane and maintaining formation at all costs, said, "In that case, I would expect to see four equally-spaced holes in the side of the mountain." As the speaker, you are the lead airplane. Your audience will go where you take them.

• *After the break.* When the audience takes a break, their minds scatter. You might have had them well-focused and concentrated during your talk, but once you release them, it is hard to restore their concentration.

I learned a technique about getting the audience focused again from the singer Lou Rawls. Apparently Lou once sang in little cabarets where it was always noisy. When he would tell a story about something that had happened to him in his life, the room would get quiet. After he had quieted the room with his story, he would begin his song.

Motivational speaker John Hammond uses another effective technique. After a break, John invites those who are listening in his audience to join him on the count of three in "sh-h-h-h-hing" the rest of the audience. No matter how large the crowd, John's technique produces silence almost immediately. What Lou Rawls, John Hammond, and others have learned is this: If you simply stand up and try to talk *over* the crowd noise, much of what you say will be lost—and it will take longer to get the crowd's attention.

Don't follow your instincts!

I've seen a lot of speakers make a bad situation even worse

because he or she felt the need to over-control. Allow yourself a brief moment, a pause, time to inhale and exhale—and you'll be much better prepared to handle your situation, whatever it is. Here are some typical problems you are likely to encounter, along with a tip on how to handle yourself:

• *Noise.* Move away from it, not toward it. Get quieter, not louder. Otherwise, it becomes a contest between you and the sound. People don't want to miss what you have to say. When you get quieter, the audience listens harder to you.

• *Sneezes.* If you are wearing a lavalier microphone, be sure to deflect the sneeze so you don't blow the sound system. The one time I sneezed into a lavalier microphone without turning away, I darn near deafened my entire audience. When I sneeze on stage, my standard line is, "I've always wondered what I would do if that happened." Then I just keep on going.

• *Colds and physical infirmities.* You must get your rest and be healthy if you are going to deliver a good presentation. If you are worn down by traveling, working all night, or too much par-tying, it's going to affect your delivery. I sometimes speak all day one day, fly all night, then speak again the next day. My schedule *invites* problems. That's why I've come to regard my physical well-being so much. The last thing you want to do is give your speech looking like Lorne Greene's dog. Do you remember him? On the dog food commercials, Loren would introduce his pet by saying, "In real people age, he's 137 years old."

• *Medications.* Stay away from them if at all possible. If I have a cold, I'd rather suffer my own personal discomfort than force my audience to suffer my medication. You won't be a very effective presenter if you are high on Contact.

• *Bloopers.* Have you ever said anything in front of a crowd and moments later wished you hadn't said it? I was speaking before a huge convention in Atlanta and covering a lot of material in a hurry when I stammered out a unique pronunciation of the phrase "to-do sheet." I'll let you use your imagination as to what it sounded like. I was embarrassed—and so was the audience!

Once you've blooped, there's no getting it back. It's out there for everyone to notice. My advice is to enjoy your boo-boos as much, if not more, than anyone else in the room. Laugh at your own faux pas louder than anyone.

• *Lights out.* If you are suddenly thrust into the dark, some folks in your audience may panic. Open the doors immediately. Send someone to check on the problem. Above all, urge the crowd to remain calm. It's possible the problem is a fire, so act cautiously and quickly. As the speaker, you need to remain in control so you can inspire the audience to do the same.

By the way, fire alarms will distract your audience in a big way. The tendency is to ignore the sound, assuming that it is a false alarm. Beware; practice safety first. You're the authority figure in a room full of human beings and the risk is just too great to ignore the alarm. Open the doors and tell your audience that although it's probably a false alarm, it's wise to make an orderly exit *just in case.* Then be traffic cop and dismiss them to leave, section by section.

• *Illness in the audience.* A medical emergency is no time to lose your composure. Take a deep breath and remind yourself that the person experiencing the illness is far more important at that moment than you or your message. If the person is able to exit the room with assistance, wait until they have left before de-escalating the situation with humor. I sometimes say, "I wonder if it was something he ate...or something I said." Be sensitive; don't say anything that might appear to be mocking the person with the medical problem.

If someone in your audience becomes unconscious, you have a major emergency on your hands. Now it's doubly important that you, as the authority figure, remain calm, composed, and take swift action. Summon paramedics, hotel security, or whoever— but get that person's needs administered to pronto! You may want to defer to the host for the evening; he or she probably knows the audience better than you and is in a better position to judge their ability to refocus on the program.

• *Hecklers.* These are people who say things just to push your buttons and get you to react. They can really threaten your equilibrium. If you pretend the heckler isn't there, he'll probably just resort to more disruptive tactics to get the attention he wants.

The route I usually follow is to acknowledge the heckler by asking him to stand and give the audience his name. It's a cinch that the audience is as annoyed as you are. By identifying the individual and bringing him into the program, you place a performance expectation on him that he wants no part of. He has no interest in becoming responsible for the presentation; he only want to disrupt your presentation. Try my suggestion. It works.

Questions and answers

Even though the question and answer time comes near the end of your presentation, just before your final few sentences, it's important not to treat this time as an afterthought or a throw-away component of the meeting. Take it seriously and follow some basic rules to make sure this time is comfortable for you, contributes to your overall performance, and is beneficial to the audience.

Always tell the audience that there will be a ten-minute maximum for questions and answers. This puts the concept of brevity in their minds before anyone opens his or her mouth. Too often, folks get up and ramble on and on without asking a direct question. Before anyone stands up, urge anyone who asks a question to be specific.

Another problem is the person who likes to hog the floor—you know, the person who needs to book a speech of his or her own. To help prevent someone from launching into a long lecture, I identify the next three people I plan to recognize for their questions. That way, the person asking the question knows that there are several other people waiting their turn to ask questions.

From time to time, you'll get a "loaded" question. If there is an inaccurate premise in a question, you need to interrupt the questioner and correct the problem. Restate the point as *you* want it to be understood.

Actually, it's a good idea to repeat and paraphrase all questions for the benefit of your audience. This is particularly needed if the question asked is very long. During the time it takes you to repeat the question, you can be thinking about how to answer—not only *what* to say, but how to say it best.

When the time you said that you would allot for questions is up, stop. No matter how many hands are in the air, tell the audience the time period has elapsed.

A good landing is essential

Sometimes the best planning can never fully prepare you for the unexpected, and you may struggle through some bumpy moments in every presentation. Management expert Peter F. Drucker said this: "A crisis must never be experienced for a *second* time." It's OK to get caught off-guard by something the first time, but you should be prepared for it in the future.

The one place you don't want to be bumpy or weak is the finish. This is the time in your presentation when it *most* important that you are well-prepared and are in complete control. The strength with which you close will have a huge impact on how memorable your speech will be.

Most strong closes are filled with conviction and emotion. This usually means that your close will be both powerful and short. It is tough to stretch passion and conviction out over a long period of time.

The basic content of your close should restate the main points you have talked about. Then briefly—but pointedly—state what it means in a way that the audience will appreciate. The Russian playwright Anton Chekov said, "If you show a gun in Act I, make sure it goes off in Act III."

Remember: Excellence takes time

Great speeches never happen by accident, even though accidents happen in great speeches. A good speaker makes giving a speech or making a presentation *look* easy, as if he or she is just having a relaxed and informative conversation with the audience. In fact, making a good presentation takes work. Mark Twain said, "It usually takes more than three weeks to prepare a good impromptu speech."

Becoming proficient at speaking will take time and practice. As I stated before, your ability to weather the storms will depend upon how much forethought and preparation you invest in your presentation.

I close every speech with four all-important words that I believe summarize the path you will need to follow if you are determined to become an excellent speaker:

1. *Dream* the great dreams. Unplug; pull out the stops; go for the top.

2. *Study* everything you can get your hands on. I spent nine years preparing to speak professionally. Investing time and effort into your presentation will improve it, no matter what your topic is.

3. *Plan* your time, and time your plan. You need to know where you are going next if you are going to get to where you want to go. You need to have a schedule as well as a destination if you are going to assess your progress.

4. *Action* is the critical element in any endeavor, especially speaking. A dream, a plan, and all the knowledge in the world are of little value if you don't act on them.

I'd like to leave you with some lines I have written about committing myself to growing and improving with every speech I make. I call these works "The Speaker's Creed":

As I stand in front of each audience, I am judged. But more importantly, I see myself as I truly am. If there is a difference between these two perceptions, then it becomes a demand for growth on my part with self-respect as the reward. I will be the person my audience believe me to be.

As I challenge and inspire others to grow and develop, I will commit to even greater personal efforts to do the same. I can never ask others to take risks I would not take. I will live my life fully and courageously as I cross from solid ground into the unknown. I will report, truthfully, the failures and successes of these adventures. I will be seen as both vulnerable and tenacious in these growth-producing experiences.

Each time I speak, I offer to my audience a small portion of the life that has made me what I am today. For that same reason, I, therefore, hold any other speaker's material as sacred, for it not only comes from the fabric of his or her own life but is delivered from the heart. I refuse to divert any one of these special and precious creations to my audience as though it were my own, lest I be withdrawing from an account to which I have made no deposits.

By virtue of the fact that I have the privilege of standing in front of a gathering of eager human minds, I will never forget that I wield the awesome, God-given power to influence the way people think. It is a responsibility that I refuse to take lightly. With truth as the foundation, I commit to continued improvement of these communication skills.

Here and now, I pledge a renewed intensity to each speech that I make. I will deliver each message as though this was my last opportunity to share what I have learned thus far in life. I will then know as I step down from each succeeding platform that that was my best effort–ever.

I challenge you to never be less than your dreams. And I wish you lots of green lights and blue skies.

After serving 10 years as a fighter pilot in the United States Air Force, Danny Cox joined a large sales company. A year later, he was promoted to manager and guided his office in a record-breaking pace. Four years later, he was promoted to vice president and assigned eight offices. By teaching the same leadership principles to the branch managers, his team shattered old sales records. As morale and productivity soared, turnover dropped to near zero. In a five-year period, production increased more than 800 percent. Due to the demand for sales and leadership techniques in other companies, Danny packed his bags—and has hardly unpacked them since.

So You've Been Asked To Give a Talk

19

Allan J. Hurst, CMC
45-175 Panorama Dr., Suite D
Palm Desert, CA 92260
619-779-1300
800-367-4873
Fax 619-779-1301

"Four Score and Seven Years Ago Our Forefathers Brought Forth . . . . " opens one of the most powerful and long remembered "talks" ever given. You and I will probably not ever have the opportunity to make such an historic speech as we pursue excellence with our own messages to audiences. The great need of our own young country at that time in history gave Abraham Lincoln a special moment to speak to the need of those citizens for reassurance that there would be a future with hope and opportunity. Such was that auspicious opening for the audience gathered at Gettysburg as they were addressed by an articulate statesman who brought his point of view to their attention.

So it is with us, as we attempt to move, sway, encourage, transfer confidence and try to make the world a better place for ourselves and all of those we touch, that we search for a similar stirring opening as the one at Gettysburg.

As powerful as an opening may be, with all the theatrics, drama and skill of the presenter, it takes third place in the order of importance when preparing a talk or speech. Third, because it is easier to choose an effective opening with a better perspective after you've prepared the other two elements. You can then focus upon the best way to catch the audience's wandering and un-focused attention when you have the other two elements devel-oped, finished and put behind you in your preparation.

In my 27 years' of experience in preparing for and delivering more than 3500 talks, I've found that the process for improving your chances of success and lowering the risk of bombing in front of newly impressed "non-friends" is a three-step process:

First, develop the close or ending of your time together with any audience. Beginning with the end in mind is the cornerstone of putting together the right message for the audience at hand. It gives them the right "taste in their mouths and minds" to reflect your, the speaker's, point-of-view. Bill Gove, in his Speech Workshop in Florida, suggests a point of view that will disturb, motivate, soothe, promote kindness and gentleness or any other action, is the starting point for a great talk. To develop this start-ing point, ask yourself the question, "What do you want the audi-ence to do, know about or think after you have finished with your time together?" This is true whether you are preparing for a 10 minute presentation or a full-day seminar. When you near the finish, give them a call to action. That is an action to write, ask another, join in, buy, study this matter further, etc., in a way that makes sense and follows the logic of your overall presentation. Art Holst is one of the best closers of all time with his poems and sayings. He has gathered them from a lifetime of refereeing pro-fessional football games and following his passion of making thousands of talks in his fifty years of platform work. Whether it is the R.L. Sharpe poem of "A Bag Of Tools," which says:

"Isn't it strange, that princes and kings,
And Clowns that caper in sawdust rings,
And common people like you and me
Are builders of eternity?

Each is given a bag of tools, a shapeless mass
A book of rules;
And each must make, ere life is flown,
A stumbling block . . . or a stepping stone."

. . . or a story of personal success or triumph over adversity, the carefully chosen poem, saying or personal vignette will give your talk wings to catch the audience up and take them to a place they could not go by themselves. This is the goal of the close.

Think of those speakers you have listened to in your lifetime that had an impact on you. And then think about how that speaker left you! It certainly had to have emotion and enthusiasm that was transferred to you. I feel sure that the greater the emotion felt by you the greater the impact. Hence, the clear memory of it today as you reflect.

You need not be a celebrity or have spent six-plus years in the Hanoi Hilton to have a background that gives you the right to speak professionally and for money. Each of you reading this book has in your past an event, an action, an experience that will move others to have hope, a good feeling of being, or add a piece to a technical puzzle that they would not have had without your choosing it as the closing point of your talk.

Second, create the body of your remarks. Why should the audience embrace your point of view? The old proverb of "Example, Point & Reason" serves well for fleshing out the content of your talk.

Here's an example of what I mean:

EXAMPLE: Always put the emphasis upon the expectation when giving an employee, associate or friend any suggestions or guidance if you want it to motivate change or alter behavior.

POINT: E2 is my memory symbol that means keep the eyes and mind focused on the next act since that is the only time frame that possesses the opportunity or hope to make improvement. Pointing out specific mistakes of someone's past only smacks of arrogance, hubris and an elevation of one's own value of self. It seldom, if ever, motivates one to improve or lead the way to more self discovery for improvement.

REASON: If everyone followed the E2 guideline then more team members would have the opportunity to focus their energies and creativity on getting the job completed in a productive manner and on a job ownership basis. Another reason to follow this guideline is that those who are thought to have a competence and don't are discovered early. Before their errors and mistakes make more work for the already generally overworked members, corrective action can be taken. Most people want to do a good job and could be members of a group of people I call "Hermans & Marthas"* who always set a standard of performance higher than anyone else would set for them. There also is a group of people in the world I call "Red Ants, Rednecks & Mavericks"* that just delight in making life more difficult and less fun for all those around them. Their delight is always at the expense of others. They are the self-ordained critics of the world and contribute only after they themselves have been satisfied.

* Contact the author for a complete explanation of these behavior groups.

This second stage of development of any talk or seminar can be punctuated with quotes that hit the mark, true success stories you have firsthand knowledge of that confirms that it can be and has been done. This is where you can use personal experiences or those of others that are creditable and clear in their message toward your point of view to build the core of your talk.

Think with your audience by showing the dilemmas you have faced by asking questions like, "How many of you have ever had a good idea shot down without a good hearing?" . . . And then wait for them to raise their hands with yours in the air. Leading the way is an example of causing them to seriously consider the point of view you are promoting. This is truly the stage that will cause those who will be in tune with you to join in and become a part of your like-minded friends.

The *third* and final element of developing your talk is to now step back and decide how to begin. You've all heard those speakers that begin by saying, "I'm really not a very good speaker . . . !" and then set out to prove that point of view! If you don't think you are a good speaker and worthy of the opportunity to inform, sway and challenge the audience in an entertaining way, then you surely won't. Think of the opening from the listener's point of view and empathize with them. What's on their mind? What did I learn in doing my homework to tailor the talk and have it not appear "canned"?

This if the gift of caring--caring enough about the audience, the time, the topic and the opportunity that you go in-depth to discover three things about the audience and their work that makes them think and maybe say to you after the talk, "You must have had some experience in our industry." Or better yet, they may think you have had a job like theirs.

Some speakers are successful starting with words put together in an unusual way like "Four Score and Seven Years," while others use stories, jokes on themselves, or any number of attention-getting techniques to bring the audience to the palm of the speaker's hand. A minister I know started many a special Sunday service by making eye contact with seemingly each and every person in the congregation before ever opening his mouth. When he did speak, everyone was focused and eager to hear what he had to say that day. It was a very effective technique and caused great admiration among all who heard him. He is still one of the most effective speakers I've ever known and demonstrates his effectiveness each time he gets up to speak.

Another goal of your opening is to overcome the elevated status that is often given to anyone who is willing and able to stand up and talk to any crowd larger than three. Trust and credibility come when the opening suggests to the audience that you are as human as they are, have experienced human challenges, have overcome them just like they have and have been able to balance those challenges into a perspective that gives encouragement to others.

In short, the opening (third element developed!) opens the oyster of each individual in the audience, prepares them to be receptive to the point of view coming later (that you have already developed and know!). You are able to determine the way it is to be delivered, where the humor should be and not be, how to build up the key points and how much drama to use. Remember that most audiences came without much self motivation and are challenging you or daring you to motivate them to action.

Well, there you have it! An approach to the secrets of speaking from one of those who are called masters of the craft. Study well those lessons you will learn from both kind and unkind audiences. They will reward you, invigorate you and disappoint you. At the same time, audiences will expect the absolute best you have to give them on any given occasion.

And remember always have a higher expectation of your mission and purpose for any talk than that of your audience. Strive always for perfection . . . but accept improvement!

Contact the Author at the address at beginning of this chapter for a copy of the form he uses.

Allan J. Hurst is president of Quorum, Ltd., a practice limited to specialized presentations. He is known for his motivational presentations to management with the ability to direct his message to the particular group at hand. One strength is to impart "real life" viewpoints in his presentation. Many describe his programs as a "positive challenge to personal growth." Mr. Hurst received his B.A. from the University of Kansas School of Business with additional graduate study in finance and marketing. He has been in a family business and is a member of Speakers Roundtable, a small group of distinguished professional speakers.

20

Discover The Speaking Power That's Inside of You

Bill Gove, CSP, CPAE
250 JFK Drive, #101
Atlantis, FL 33462
407-964-5225

I have visited with most of the National Speakers Association chapters around the country, and during the question-and-answer session that follows my talk, one question comes up most of the time. "Bill," they ask, "how long have you been in this business?" My answer is always the same: "I have been in the speaking business a little over 80 years."

There's usually a long silence after that response. That's when I add, "Let me explain."

My mother and father separated when I was about three years old, and I went to live with an aunt. My aunt went through four husbands in five years. Who was it that said, "I never met a man I didn't like"? Was it Will Rogers? Well, I find nothing unusual about that sentiment. I had an aunt who felt exactly the same way.

Every time she got married, we moved. And every time we moved, I was always the new kid on the block, saying, "Look at me. I'm a somebody. Pay attention."

Now that's the down side of my childhood. The up side is that my Uncle Phil—who I think was my fourth uncle—was a magnificent storyteller. He had worked in the Maine woods up on the Canadian border all his life and could tell wonderful stories using a German dialect...using a Swedish dialect...using a French Canadian dialect. When I was a little boy, I sat on Uncle Phil's lap, listened to his stories, and learned most of them.

Years later, I left home and joined the 3M Company. My first assignment included traveling with three other managers to all the branch offices to introduce new products. I was responsible for doing a half-hour speech on closing the sale. When this assignment began, I had never made a speech. Keep in mind, also, that I was assigned to speak before three managers who happened to be my bosses.

I was terrified. One half-hour on closing? Give me a break! So what I did was to develop a talk that included five minutes on closing. I filled the next 25 minutes with Uncle Phil's stories.

That was 48 years ago, and I've been doing the same thing ever since. I left 3M in 1955, and went on my own. For the rest of the 1950s, for all of the 1960s, all of the 1970s, and all of the 1980s, I was doing 150 talks a year. I used material from my 3M experiences and, of course, I told my uncle's stories.

Make a point---tell a story. Make a point---tell a story. Thank you, Uncle Phil, wherever you are. I love you.

You and your audience, together

During those years when I was making 150 talks a year, I learned a lot of things that really helped me. Things that helped me when I followed a three-hour cocktail party. Things that helped when I faced an audience that Charlie Jarvis used to describe as "a tree full of owls." From all the things that I learned, there are two that stand out in my mind as being particularly helpful to me, so I'd like to share them with you. But before I get specific on those two things, I want to tell you something I learned that changed my whole attitude about speaking. It concerns the audience.

In the beginning, I saw the audience as something to work over. I wanted to dazzle them with my verbal skills. Well, at some point in time, I began to see the audience as part of my very own support system. I don't know when this happened, but I'll tell you this: When it happened, for the first time in my career, I stopped talking at people and started talking with them.

I got to the point where I could put laughs, applause, and standing ovations on the back burner where they belong. And I started to see every talk I gave as something I gave together with the audience. Together. No more nervousness, no more stress, no more fear. Just doing what I loved to do together with the audience. I'll tell you, when you get this into your consciousness, the birds will begin to sing. I guarantee it.

Soon after I began to see speaking as something I did together with my audiences, this whole thing started to pay off. The phone started to ring. The meeting planners began calling. So many good things started to happen. It was about this time that I decided speaking was something I just had to do for the rest of my life.

How to collect material

"OK," you say, "You've told us some things that have happened along the way, Bill. But how do you get ready for a speech? Where do you get your material?"

Well, let me say first that I am in this business full time. This is my life. Because it is part of my personality and my personal philosophy to spend every waking hour totally absorbed in the moment, I am always thinking about speaking. I see a particular piece of material or hear a conversation, and I immediately think about how I might use it. Is it funny? Is it is something I might want to share with others? Does it challenge some long-held assumption that I have been protecting that has to do with me, others, my world? I'm always saying to myself, "Stay awake, Gove. Life is going on all around you." Robin Williams said it in the movie *Dead Poet's Society*. "Carpe Diem." Seize the day!

In fact, I am persuaded that this activity—the collecting of things to talk about—is the easiest part of the whole process. I mean, there is no dearth of goodies out there waiting to be translated into "bite-sized moments" that can then be converted into speech form. Emphasizing life experiences—the things that I have done that have worked for me—is what my audiences all want to hear about.

For additional material, there's the library. Let's say you have spent your lifetime up to the present working on "time management" or something like that. Now you want to go out and tell others about what you know, right? Well, the library is chock-full of books having to do with what others have done on the subject. This, added to what you already know, is more than enough good stuff to give you real content for a good speech. Oh, yes—there are also audio and video tape albums available that cover every strategy known to man, from remembering names and faces to how to build a nuclear bomb in your bathtub. Are you into negotiating and want to build a talk about it? All the stuff you need and more is yours for the asking. All you have to do is stay awake. Honest.

Oh, I know, I've had speakers at the NSA convention tell me, "Easy for you to say, Bill, but you seem to have funny things happen to you. Nothing exciting ever happens to me." Well, I have to say to them, "Truth is, the same things happen to you that happen to me. We're both on the same planet, for heaven's sake. Interesting things seem to track me down because—and this is it, I think—because I expect them to! My antennae are always up. I am always thinking, "Come on, world. I need some new stuff. Hit me, baby. I'm ready!"

There is an opening line in an old Down East Maine cookbook that my aunt used to show to me. The book was printed around the turn of the century. The recipe was for rabbit stew, and the opening sentences said, "Want to make some great rabbit stew? First, you gotta shoot a rabbit!" So if you want to put together a great speech, first you gotta stay awake.

Write it down

There have been things happening to you every day of your life that are worth sharing, and there will be new ones coming today and tomorrow. So that you won't forget any more good material, I make this very important suggestion: Whenever you see or hear anything that might be repeatable, write it down!

I keep a journal. Most of the busy speakers I know keep journals. I'll tell you, with me, if I forget to write it down, then I forget what I forgot to write down!

Dr. Charlie Jarvis, whom I quoted earlier and who is one of my favorite speakers, used to be a dentist in San Marcos, Texas. Charlie told me that once a patient came in and asked, "Doc, what do you do for yellow teeth?" Jarvis said, "Wear a brown tie." I wrote it down.

The same Dr. Jarvis wrote me a note on my last birthday. The note said, "83 is not old if you happen to be a tree." I wrote it down.

I pick up a lot of choice stuff from my breakfast club every morning. We were talking about memory and, as we grow older, we tend to forget names and places. One of our group, who has had three very serious heart operations, told us that in 1990 he forgot April. I wrote it down.

Hal Osborne said, "Sending out direct mail and then waiting at the phone for business to come in is like leaving the porch light on for Jimmy Hoffa." I wrote it down.

Ken Seaquist was talking about someone who had the reputation for finding fault. Ken said, "He's the kind of guy who would go to a sex orgy and complain about the cheese dip." I wrote it down.

Al Williams just had a pacemaker transplant. He said it needs service. Every time he feels romantic, the garage door opens. I wrote it down.

So as I said, everything you ever need to create a good speech—including your own life experiences that come out of everything you have ever seen or heard or felt—are all right there for you. Sure, you have to convert those ideas and experiences into speech form, then memorize the speech and choreograph it. But a memorable speech is out there waiting for you to find it and to give it. Compared to those who thought all those ideas up in the first place, your job is a lead-pipe cinch.

Writing isn't speaking

Now that we've got our stuff together—in our heads, in note-books, on cassettes, in shoe boxes, written on the sleeves of our shirts, or wherever—here's my second important lesson for you: Material written to be heard is different from material that is written to be read.

Too many speakers, when preparing for a meeting, sit down with a lined pad and a pen or pencil or a typewriter and go at it. And that is dangerous. Because most of the time, when we write anything, we tend to be content-oriented and information-driven. Content-oriented speeches are usually easy to read but not easy to listen to. So, instead of writing a speech, what you usually write is material that starts on page one and winds up 35 or 40 pages later and which actually is not a speech but an article, a paper, or a book report.

What has worked for me through the years is to write a speech in much the way I created my early speeches: Make a point...tell a story. Except I might vary that a little to say it like this: Make a point...use a "vignette."

Simply put, a vignette is a "for instance." An example in story form. It supports the key point the speaker has just made, supports it with people talking with people in different places under different circumstances. Most of the speakers that I've known—those who have endured in this business—are remembered by the vignettes that they use.

I suggest that you write vignettes that are six or seven minutes in length. Each one of these vignettes will have a life of its own. And, each vignette will have what all full-length speeches have: a premise, a problem, and a payoff.

It's a funny thing about vignettes. Although I've told some of them so often in my speeches that I'm a little bored with them, if

I leave one of them out, someone in the audience will say, "Why didn't you tell the Marco Island story?" They seem to remember the example first, then the key point second.

Rely on your natural self

So, to wrap it up, I advise all who want to be better speakers to stay awake to life. All you need to make your presentation really sing is out there waiting for you to find it. Material written to be heard is different from material written to be read; speeches that are 100 percent content-driven don't seem to get it done. The vignette system works for me and for every busy speaker I know. That's my wisdom for you in a nutshell.

There are those who say that speaking is the toughest of all the performing arts. Don't believe it. All you have to do is take your natural self to a higher level of consciousness, and you can do it—and do it well.

Each year, Toastmasters International presents its prestigious Golden Gavel Award to an individual of significance in the field of communication and leadership. In presenting the 1995 Golden Gavel Award to Bill Gove, TI called him "an outstanding seminar leader and marketing expert who epitomizes the art of public speaking. Billed as 'a speaker's speaker,' this silver-tongued professional orator has reached the pinnacle of his profession and won the acclaim of his peers." Bill Gove is trainer, teacher, and entertainer who has an impressive record of more than 5,000 speaking engagements to leading organizations and corporations nationwide. A former executive with 3M Company, he was the first president of the National Speakers Association and is a winner of NSA's coveted Cavett Award as well as numerous other awards.

If You Care, If You Prepare, You Too Can Be A Speaking Success

21

Brian Tracy
Brian Tracy International
462 Stevens Avenue, Suite 202
Solana Beach, CA 92075
619-481-2977
800-542-4252
Fax 619-481-2445

The course of human history and personal destiny has been changed more by the spoken word than by the written word. Many of the major turning points in your own life came when someone said something to you that affected you so profoundly that ever afterwards your thinking, your feelings, and your actions were different.

It's been estimated that your ability to communicate with others, and their ability to communicate with you, is responsible for fully 85 percent of your personal success in life. There are few things more important than for you to become really, really good at the art and science of expressing yourself in words to other people.

I have spoken to many thousands of people, ranging from a group of one or two people up to 5,000 people and more. I've spoken for periods ranging from five minutes to four or five days.

I've read dozens of books and articles on professional speaking, and I've spent many thousands of hours on my feet in front of critical public audiences.

In the next few pages, I'd like to share with you some of the most important ideas I've learned in the art of public speaking. I'll give you proven ideas that you can use, starting immediately, to become more effective and more persuasive in your interactions with others, one-on-one, in small groups or with larger audiences.

At my seminars around the country, people often come up to me and say, "I would like to do what you do. How do I get started?"

Whenever someone asks me how they can become a public speaker, I always refer them to the words of Elbert Hubbard, who said, "The only way to learn to speak is to speak and speak, and speak and speak, and speak and speak, and speak." Speaking is an art, but it's an art you can learn. Like many of the keys to success, it takes a little bit of inspiration—and a lot of work.

The starting point: caring about your audience

The Dean of American public speakers, Dr. Kenneth MacFarland, who died a few years ago, wrote a book entitled, *Eloquence in Public Speaking.* In this book, he did not talk about methodology or technique at all. His central message, which really impressed me when I began speaking publicly, was that the key to eloquence was the conviction and the depth of feeling that the speaker brought to the subject.

To put it another way, the starting point of being excellent as a speaker is for you to really care about your subject.

I watched Wally "Famous Amos" Amos give a talk a couple of years ago. He had started with very little and gone on to build an extraordinarily successful chain of chocolate chip cookie stores. He has since devoted much of his time and money to helping people who are less fortunate, especially those having problems with illiteracy.

Wally Amos was not necessarily an accomplished professional speaker, but the talk that he gave was absolutely excellent. And the reason was because he spoke from his heart. He spoke with a deep concern and compassion about the needs of people who couldn't read. He wanted to get across to the audience how important it was that everyone be concerned about this subject, not only for the individuals involved, but for the future of America as a competitive nation. His eloquence came from deep inside because he really cared about his subject. Everyone listening could sense his emotions even though his structure and his style may not have been as polished as someone who had spoken for many years.

So the starting point of the art of public speaking is for you to pick a subject that you really care about. It is for you to think through the subjects that have had an inordinate impact on you, the subjects that you would like to share with others because you really, intensely feel that others could benefit from your knowledge.

Let's say, for example, that you feel that people could be far more successful in life if they learned how to be more understanding of others. You have found, in your own life, that the more you worked at understanding where others were coming from, the more effective you were in interacting and communicating with them. Because of the impact that this knowledge has had on your life, you feel that others could benefit from learning and practicing what you have learned and practiced. With this beginning, you have a springboard from which you can leap into your first public talk.

Prepare until it's "just right"

The second part of public speaking, the real core of the subject, is preparation. Preparation is more important than anything else—except caring about your subject.

Ernest Hemmingway once wrote that, "In order to write well, you must know 10 words about the subject for every word that you write. Otherwise," he said, "the reader will know that this is not true writing." I personally feel that, in speaking, you must know 100 words for every word that you speak. Otherwise, your audience will have the sense that you don't really know what you're talking about.

It's not unusual for a person who makes an excellent presentation to spend many hours, days and even weeks, preparing for a talk.

My good friend, Nido Qubein, gave a ten-part, one-hour talk, to several hundred members of the National Speakers Association about three years ago in Atlanta, Georgia. This talk was on the future of the speaking industry in the 1990's and beyond. The talk was scheduled to run for one hour, and it started and ended in about 59 minutes and 55 seconds.

Nido talked without notes. He developed each of the 10 parts of the talk sequentially and in perfect order. Each of the 10 sections contrasted a pair of principles that had to do with marketing, sales, and promotion. Each of these parts was carefully developed. Each observation was both insightful and thought-provoking.

As he spoke, Nido moved back and forth across the speaking platform. He gave specific examples and anecdotes to illustrate each point that he was making. He impressed me and the entire audience with the depth of his knowledge and with the thoroughness of his preparation.

Watching Nido's presentation, you had the feeling that he had given the talk 100 times before. He was relaxed, genial and very friendly throughout. He smiled and used his arms and his body very effectively to convey key points and illustrate and emphasize the message he was conveying. It was a beautiful example of professional speaking.

I later learned that, even though the talk was meant to be given only once, Nido had spent more than 100 hours of preparation over a period of two to three months prior to the talk, getting it to the point where it was "just right." Whenever you see a professional speaker who gives a talk that seems almost effortless, you can be very sure that it was preceded by enormous preparation.

A good friend of mine, a professional trainer, told me a story recently about a training and speaking experience he had had. He had been in the field for several years and had become so confident that he had gone in front of an important business audience with only a couple of hours of preparation for a half-day talk. He felt his knowledge of the subject would enable him to pull it off without anyone realizing that he had not done the individual, in-depth preparation that is necessary for this kind of a presentation.

To make the story short, the presentation was a disaster. Within a few minutes, he knew that he was in trouble. In a few more minutes, the audience knew that he wasn't fully prepared, and they were both insulted and angry. By the end of the first hour, the session had evolved into a series of angry questions, criticisms, disagreements and arguments that took up the rest of the morning. It was a disaster, caused solely because my friend had neglected to prepare before going in.

The next time my friend was given the opportunity to make a presentation in front of a business audience, he spent every spare moment the week before, preparing and organizing fastidiously, in advance. This time, he was ready. The presentation went off without a hitch. He received rave reviews and commentaries from the audience. Afterwards, he told me that failing to prepare for the previous talk was one of the most valuable lessons he had ever learned. He would never again make the mistake of thinking that he could get by simply with knowledge of the subject.

Start with an objective statement

To prepare for a talk, the first thing you should do is write out an objective statement of what you wish to accomplish as a result of this presentation. If it's a ten-minute presentation, or a ten-hour presentation, the statement of your objective is the same. It's the answer to the question, "Who is my audience and what effect do I want my talk to have upon them?"

Ralph Waldo Emerson once wrote, "The aim of all public speaking is to move the listeners to take action of some kind, action that they would not have taken in the absence of your words." So you need to ask, "What action do I want this audience to take as the result of the things I say to them?"

Write out this action statement of objectives very clearly in advance. Then, write down everything that you think you could possibly say, one after the other, to this audience to cause them to take this action. Remember, the reason for public speaking is not to simply teach or to share information. It's to move people's minds and hearts and to motivate them into changing their behavior in some way.

Research your subject in depth

Once you have an outline of what you want to accomplish and some of the ways that you can accomplish it, begin to do your research. If you don't have enough information, begin to read, review, and ask questions.

For example, never assume that you already know everything you need to know. Another friend of mine was asked to give a talk on the importance of strategic thinking, something that he felt very strongly about, but a subject on which he had not done very much reading. He was amazed to find that it took him two solid weeks of reading and taking notes to get enough information together to give a one-hour talk on strategic thinking.

When you begin to talk, you'll be amazed at how much background work you'll have to do, even on a subject with which you're relatively familiar, before you're in a position to stand up in front of people and speak fluently on the issue. Remember, you need to know 100 words for every word that you say. You need to have read at least 100 words for every word that goes into the talk that you give to an audience. If you've not done this quantity of research, both you and the audience will know it very quickly.

If you're giving a short talk, the very best strategy I've found is for you to write out your thoughts, word for word, in detail. Then, read the material you've written and edit it. Revise it wherever necessary. Add to it and subtract unnecessary data. Work on it until it is polished, then read it through several times so that you have such a good sense for the material that you can go through the whole talk prior to falling asleep or while you're driving in your car.

Not long ago, I was invited to give a keynote talk of 22 minutes to a world-class audience of more than 5,000 professionals. The organizers asked me for a written outline of the talk, which they planned to carefully review and critique before giving me the go-ahead to put it into its final form for presentation to their audience.

Although I knew the subject intimately, it took me many hours to write and re-write the script for this talk. I then gave the talk to a special audience of reviewers from this organization. They gave me about 20 ideas on how to expand or improve the talk in some way. I then re-wrote the talk a final time and submitted it to the organizers for their approval. Only then did I get the go-ahead to give the talk to the audience of 5,000 sales executives a few months hence.

Once the talk had been finalized, I reviewed it more than 50 times, memorizing the entire talk so that I could give it from my heart rather than simply trying to remember the words and paragraphs. The net effect of all of this preparation was that the talk brought a standing ovation from 5,000 people, and I was afterwards told that it was the finest talk ever presented to that organization in their 37-year history.

It was no miracle. Every single additional hour of preparation had paid off. In fact, preparation is fully 90 percent of your success in public speaking. You may not have the platform skills of a great orator, but you can be an extremely effective speaker if you really do your homework thoroughly in advance.

Practice, the key to perfection

If the first two parts of successful public speaking are caring and preparing, the third part is practice. You need to practice your talk, over and over, in front of friends, relatives, members of your family and even in front of a mirror.

If you have a tape recorder—or even better, a movie camera—record or video yourself giving the talk from end to end. Then listen to your delivery or watch it, and make notes on how you could make it better. If you're using a video camera, look into the camera and use the same facial expressions and the same bodily gestures that you would if you were speaking directly to another person. When you critique yourself, be very hard on yourself. Remember, the more honest and objective you can be about how you come across to others, the more effective you'll be when you finally get on your feet.

Practice makes perfect, and perfect practice makes it even more perfect. This reminds me of a true story concerning my daughter, Christina, who was 10 years old at the time of the incident.

She was attending a private school near our home. The school wanted to build on a new addition, but they were rebuffed by a neighborhood committee that got together to join a town council meeting and loudly disagreed with the issuing of a building permit. The members of the council had no choice but to put the permit into suspension.

The founders of the school asked me if I would help them prepare a presentation to the city council in order to make a second attempt to get the building permit. I told them that I would work with them but that the entire presentation would have to be very carefully prepared and organized in advance. Previously, they had just walked into the city council chambers against an entrenched opposition and had been defeated hands-down.

While we were going through this preparation, Christina said that she wanted to ask the city council members to approve the permit. She actually wanted to speak at a public hearing. I told her that she could but she would have to write out her talk, word for word, and memorize it, if she wanted to get a chance to speak on such an important matter.

Before the week was out, she had gotten together with her babysitter and my wife and had written out a complete five minute presentation. She then read and reviewed it, over and over again and, before the city council meeting came up, she was able to stand in front of the family and deliver her speech, word for word, without notes.

On the evening of the city council meeting, various adults gave parts of the planned presentation and were quite effective. But perhaps the turning point in the entire process was when Christina stood up on a chair, behind the speaker's rostrum, and gave her talk, ending with the words, "Please pass this application and allow us to build a new school."

Well, the effect was incredible. Even though there were many residents of the surrounding neighborhood who got up and spoke against the application, the city council voted and approved it. There were more than 130 adults in the audience, including representatives of two local newspapers. The following day, Christina Tracy was written up on the front pages of both newspapers as the 10-year old girl who had given a talk in public to support the application.

Working to improve pays off

Remember, your ability to speak effectively in front of other people can do more to advance your career and your life than perhaps any other skill you can develop.

It's normal and natural for you to be nervous about public speaking. Fifty-four percent of American adults place public speaking ahead of fear of death amongst life's major fears. Most people find that their hearts pound and they become nervous and uneasy with the very thought of standing up and speaking in front of an audience.

However, you can overcome this fear, just as you can learn to type with a typewriter or ride a bicycle. You can take a course from Dale Carnegie, or you can join your local chapter of Toastmasters. These organizations put you through a process of what psychologists call "systematic desensitization." What this means is that at every meeting, you get a chance to stand up and speak. Eventually, you learn that you don't need to have any fear or uneasiness about the process. Within six months, you'll be quite accomplished at picking a topic, organizing your material, and presenting the subject effectively within a specific time period.

And this is not really a skill that you can take or leave. If you want to realize your full potential in the world of business, you must learn how to be effective with other people. I have seen executives make extraordinary career jumps, saving themselves as much as five to ten years of working up the executive ladder, simply by speaking extremely effectively in front of their peers at a corporate meeting. I've seen and observed men and women who have put their careers onto the fast track by overcoming their fears and learning how to speak persuasively to others.

Not long ago, a gentleman came up to me at one of my seminars and asked me if I remembered him. I told him that I didn't. He went on to remind me that a year ago he had attended one of my seminars in which I had recommended that people learn how to speak effectively on their feet if they wanted to get ahead in their careers.

At that time, he said, he was terrified of the very idea of speaking in front of a group. He also realized, as he listened to me, that his fear of speaking in front of others was holding him back, while people of less competence than he were moving ahead in his company simply because they weren't afraid to give presentations to clients. He resolved at that moment that he was going to learn how to speak.

This man went out of the seminar, picked up the telephone book, and joined a local chapter of Toastmasters International. He began to go to their meetings every week. Within a few months he was becoming quite competent at speaking to groups. And, as it always happens, his boss came up to him one day and asked if he would give a presentation to a client group because his boss wasn't able to go. He accepted this assignment with some trepidation, but he went anyway.

The night before, the man spent several hours preparing thoroughly for the presentation. When he arrived at the site for the presentation, he felt fairly calm and confident and in control of himself. He gave an excellent presentation. By the time he got back to the office, the client had telephoned his boss and thanked them for sending such a well-prepared and excellent speaker to share this information with them.

"Now," he told me, "my company sends me out to client corporations at least twice a week. I've received two raises in salary, and I'm already earning 40 percent more than I was a year ago. And I owe it all to your advice and to my learning how to speak on my feet."

So I give this same advice to you: Pay any price, spend any amount of time, overcome any obstacle, but make a decision, right now, that you're going to learn to speak well to other people. It could be one of the most important decisions you ever make in assuring your long-term success in your career.

Brian Tracy has been called a "motivational superstar" and an "inspirational guru" by leading magazines. He is one of the world's foremost authorities on individual and organizational success. His fast-moving talks on sales, personal achievement, and leadership are stimulating, entertaining, and thought-provoking. Brian Tracy speaks to more than 100,000 people worldwide each year.

Speaking Is Simple: **22**
Just Tell People
What You Know

Ira M. Hayes CPAE

1921 - 1995

A rich woman walked up to the golf pro at an expensive resort and said, "I'd like for you to teach my friend here how to play golf."

"Fine," said the pro, "but how about you?"

"Oh, I learned yesterday!" she replied.

I share that funny story with you here to illustrate that learning to be a good speaker is something like learning to play golf. You can't master it all in one day–or even in one year. I should know. It took me years of learning and more years of practice to become good at speaking. But I can also tell you that, like golf, speaking is a skill that you can learn.

I didn't become a professional speaker because I was gifted at speaking. In fact, I became a speaker quite by accident.

I sold cash registers for the National Cash Register Company for about eight years early in my career. During these years,

I created and developed some unique selling techniques that worked successfully for me, and my company asked me to take a special assignment, going across the United States and Canada presenting these ideas to the company's entire sales force. That's how my speaking career began, just talking to people about the things I knew. Actually, that was a good way to begin, because a good speech or presentation should be like a one-to-one talk about something that both the speaker and the listener are interested in.

I did my programs for nearly 39 years. It's my hope that the things I learned and summarize here will be of help to you.

The No. 1 rule for success

To make an effective speech, you must have something to say. There are many different things that people may have to say that would put them in the position of standing in front of an audience. The speaker might be asked to make a sales presentation or to address a civic group. Perhaps you need to address a church audience or the membership of a club. Or maybe you just need to give a committee report. In each of these cases, you should have something to say that will benefit your audience. No amount of technique will make up for empty content.

Building blocks

Over the years, I've seen thousands of people stand in front of many different kinds of audiences, and I have concluded that the best presentations and speeches are built on a foundation of certain key building blocks. I can identify eight of these blocks that help build a successful presentation.

- The obvious one: Be informative.
- Be valuable. That is, share something that benefits your audience.
- Be interesting.
- Be enjoyable.
- Be memorable.
- Be believable.

• Strive to be inspirational.
• Be professional.

It may not, of course, be possible to display all of these qualities in every speech, but the more you can incorporate, the better your presentation will be. In my opinion, three elements that you should be able to achieve in *every* presentation are:

1. Be informative.
2. Be valuable.
3. Be memorable.

Share information

What information can you convey to your audience? What do they want or need to know? What do you know that may help them grow better at what they do, or inspire them, or motivate them? What do you have to say that will enrich their lives?

Once you identify what you want to share with your audience, the next step is to organize your material. I've found a good rule of thumb in writing a speech or in organizing material is to think in terms of the following:

• What's happened in the past?
• What's happening now?
• How will your information or material help the listener in the future?

To get started in organizing material or information, I find it helpful to take several sheets of tablet-size paper (8" x 10" size) and jot down one idea or pertinent bit of information on each individual, separate sheet of paper. Try to cover every point or item you think is important.

The reason for putting these individual ideas or bits of information on separate sheets of paper is that it allows you to physically move the paper around until you find the smoothest, most logical sequence for presenting each idea or bit of information. Keep in mind that your goal is to present your ideas so that they are clear and your audience can easily follow as you share your ideas with them. My usual procedure is to arrange all the individual pieces of paper on the floor or on a desk, moving them around until I create the sequence I believe is best.

As you prepare a speech or presentation, think of it as a roadmap. You have a starting point and a destination. Let's look for the shortest and most interesting way to get from the start to the finish.

Opening and closing

Make sure that your appearance and your opening remarks will give you the greatest possible chance for the audience to accept you favorably and believe what you are telling them. In your opening remarks, explain the basic reason for being with the audience and the main point of your presentation. Most of the time, this can be done in a simple way. Here's an example:

"Good morning. I'm so happy to have this opportunity to talk with you about the outstanding accomplishments of your engineering department."

Plan your opening remarks to get favorable attention. In almost every presentation, the speaker is attempting to get the audience to eventually agree with him or her, or to accept the speaker's ideas, or to take action on what is presented. This becomes the body of the presentation and ends with the close of the speech.

Try to keep the body of your presentation simple. Don't get too complicated. Don't use too many statistics. An easy way to present the facts and ideas in the body of the presentation is to use comparisons and/or to illustrate your points with experience stories.

Now for the close. Don't drag it out. Summarize specifically what you want your audience to do, or remember, or believe. End with enthusiasm, and convey a sense of thankfulness for being invited to speak before the group.

The visual factor

We have touched briefly on the major factors of making a presentation. Your material is now arranged in the best possible way. You have written an interesting opening; you have your facts well-placed; you have included comparisons and experience stories; you have fashioned a good close. Now you need to be sure the audience remembers what you have said.

One of the ways to increase the odds that your presentation will be remembered is through the use of visual aids. It is believed that the eye is 22 times more powerful than the ear in the retention of information. For visual impact, you can use slides, overheads, charts, or a combination of words and visual props.

Over the years, I have stressed the importance of "Conformity" by using a colorful card (about 20 inches by 5 inches). It has a little easel on the back so that I can stand it up on the table for the audience to see. Along with this sign, I have a real Davy Crockett coonskin cap that I hold up and explain that when my son was a youngster, he wanted a Davy Crockett hat because everyone else already had one. I also had a large cartoon of a youngster wearing the hat. This was displayed on an easel as one of many charts I used throughout the program. Words, a coonskin cap, a sign, and a large cartoon—a lot of visuals, I agree, but I know from remarks made to me later that people did not miss or forget my message. Visuals helped to make it memorable.

Suggesting the use of visual aids seems elementary, yet only a small percentage of presenters in front of any given audience will use any kind of visual aid. In addition to helping the audience remember your message, visual aids also make your presentation more enjoyable and interesting.

Experience stories

Give as much of your information and material as you can in the form of experience stories. An experience story simply means giving information to the audience as you would to a friend in conversation. Here's an example I often use:

"I had just returned home from a long, tiring week and our son ran out to meet me hollering, 'Dad, we have to go right downtown to the store to get something that's an emergency!' (He wanted that Davy Crockett hat!)"

Experience stories hold the audience's attention. The opposite of the experience story would be cold facts or dry statistics. It's important to include facts in many presentations, but you can always use comparisons that the audience can identify with. For example, if you were trying to show the power of the F-16 fighter aircraft, it would be much more meaningful to say, "The F-16 fighter plane has the same power as 65 Indianapolis racing cars tied together."

Looking professional

A truly professional speaker would make the presentation totally from memory. However, most people would not be in this category, so it is perfectly normal and acceptable to use notes or a written script.

Many speeches are given by an individual simply reading the script, word for word. If you must do it this way, have the script typed in BIG, **Bold** type. Triple space the lines so you can comfortably read a sentence. Mark your place on the script with your finger. Look up at the audience. Then look down and read a few more lines.

Naturally, you will look much more professional if you don't have to read your speech. One technique is to take a single piece of paper and, in a series of blocks, highlight the main points you want to make. Use just key words or ideas. You can then talk with your audience, having good eye contact, and only occasionally look down at your notes.

One thing that can detract from your professional appearance is nervousness. Inexperienced speakers have a tendency, because of nervousness, to unconsciously do annoying things such as rocking back and forth from one foot to another, tapping on the lectern with a pencil, jingling a bunch of coins in a pocket, constantly clearing their throat, or using repetitive words such as "You will note..." or "You know..." Here's a simple answer to a few of those problems: Don't have pencils or coins or other things you won't need on the lectern with you.

Nervousness is a common problem for the new or occasional speaker. In fact, in a survey presented in *The Book of Lists,* fear of getting up and speaking in front of a group topped the list of the 14 major fears of the human race. This is understandable, since most of us are afraid of what is new or unknown to us.

Practice builds confidence

It will help you tremendously to rehearse, and rehearse, and rehearse again your material. Practice giving it until you know it thoroughly. Really think about the words you are going to say. And don't tell your audience you are nervous.

Experience builds confidence. If you continue to do much speaking or presentations, you'll recognize that with experience, speaking becomes easier. Remember, speaking is a skill most people can learn.

Another way to calm your nerves is to check and re-check everything you will be using in your presentation. Many things can go wrong to make you look bad or upset you, so prepare a little checklist of all your props and material. Are your slides in order? Are they all in the proper position? Any upside-down or backwards? Can everyone in the audience see and read the words or figures? Is the lectern the right height for you? Check the microphone.

Don't ever take anything for granted. Remember, anything that can happen *will* happen, and the smallest thing that happens might ruin your presentation.

The good speaker inside of you

Great speakers are not born; many of the best professional

speakers discover their talent later in their careers. You may be one of the rare individuals who has the special talents required to become a truly inspirational speaker.

What is the secret to being inspirational? Inspiration reflects overwhelming belief in what you want your audience to hear. And also, the overwhelming desire on the speaker's part is for the audience to benefit by this deeply-believed message or information.

Why not put together a little presentation about something you are familiar with? Practice it. Present it to your family or friends. Go back over it and check to see if you have covered the major steps we've talked about here. Remember, speaking is a skill. If you review this chapter regularly, and practice, chances are high that you will become a better speaker than you are right now.

Ira Hayes joined NCR Corporation as a salesman. He rose quickly within the company, eventually becoming head of NCR's advertising and promotion department. As part of his staff duties, Ira began speaking to business groups, and his energetic, upbeat presentations earned him the honorary title "Ambassador of Enthusiasm." In 1979, Ira founded his own company and began speaking professionally. His in-depth knowledge of selling, advertising, and personal motivation brought him recognition as one of the top motivational speakers in America. Ira has performed at more than 4,000 meetings and has been seen, either live or via movies or video tape, by more than three million people. He is the author of *Yak, Yak, Yak,* a book on speaking, and *Success: Go For It.* He is a past president of the National Speakers Association (NSA) and has received the NSA's most cherished recognition, the Cavett Award.

Epilogue

by Ron Arden

For the past several years, I have had the remarkable opportunity of being coach to the members of Speakers Roundtable. As their coach, even as I shared my skills with them, there's much I have learned in return. This group of remarkable people with extraordinary talent is immensely selfless and, as you have discovered reading this book, they are willing to share with each other and those who seek them out all that they have harvested over their many years on the platform.

Never has information been so freely available as it is today. Whether through the newspaper, radio, television, audio and video tapes, books, or computers and the Internet, the information highway is becoming crowded to the breaking point. But, the more and more information there is "out there," the less and less valuable much of it becomes. We just don't have time to sort amongst the choices, decide, and then absorb it all.

But, when you take information and process it through personal experience, it becomes knowledge, and it's value increases tremendously. Nevertheless, knowledge too is freely available. Just think of all the "How To," "Teach Yourself," and "Self Improvement" books, lectures, seminars, and the like that are available on demand. Now if someone takes all this information and knowledge and distills it into a fine visceral and intellectual "brandywine," then you have a product that is perhaps the most valuable on earth—wisdom. What is contained in this book is hundreds of years of art and wisdom.

For you, the reader, to extrapolate from the contents of this book what may best serve you, let me make this suggestion. The styles and talents of this great group of speakers are all unique.

Seek out the qualities, techniques, and values they all have in common—those things you have come across repeatedly. Use these commonalities as a guide, because it is in the similarities that their true "secrets" are revealed.

Let me issue this warning: If you attempt to copy or imitate their uniqueness, which is a product of the many factors that create their persona, you will likely become an empty, hollow clone. You will risk the loss of your own true identify and therewith your credibility. Without credibility, a speaker is nothing. You must discover and develop your own uniqueness.

As for my experience with Speakers Roundtable members, I want to share with you what I have discovered to be true of them all. Every one of the members is a behaviorist, philosopher, educator, psychologist, and mini-cynic who loves life and people desperately. They all have boundless energy that they modulate so that it doesn't become oppressive. They know how to cunningly "play" their audience so they constantly engage and re-engage their minds and hearts. They are visionaries who see where most of us cannot see.

They have learned which intellectual switches to trip in order to engage the minds of audience members and what emotional buttons to press that will trigger an audience's feelings.They are smart enough to understand that wisdom is a tool kit they leave behind with their audiences, but that it is emotion that gives their audiences the wherewithal to use the tools. They know what I call "The Ten Commandments of Successful Presentations"—one through five are "Know Thy Audience," six through nine are "Know Thyself," and ten is "Know Thy Stuff."

So, observe closely, objectively, and passionately life, nature, and we who people this globe. Take the information from your ongoing observations of life and your endless discovery of people's behavior, then live it all into knowledge. Take a little time to condense, encapsulate, and crystallize it all into wisdom.

Finally, remember to create from the heart and the mind together, and learn how to always communicate both with skill. Then, reread these chapters again and again and again.

Speech Dynamics
3728 Dixon Place
San Diego, CA 92107
619-222-1499

Ron Arden is widely regarded as one of the leading and most versatile image and communication consultants on the West Coast. He has developed an innovative approach to helping clients create an appropriate image, both personal and corporate, through persuasive and impactful communication techniques. His concepts are based on the latest research into interpersonal communication, his own background in education and theatre, and his wide professional experience. Ron Arden is a former professor of theatre, theatre director, and adjunct professor in trial practice presentation skills. He holds two teaching degrees from Trinity College, London, England. He has been a valuable professional resource to Speakers Roundtable for a number of years.

World Headquarters
P.O. Box 9052
Mission Viejo, CA 92690
(714) 858-8255

The Toastmasters International program is for everyone 18 years of age or older who wants to develop their ability to communicate confidently. There are more than 7,500 Toastmasters clubs around the world. They meet at breakfast, lunch and in the evenings in corporations and communities of all types. No invitation is needed in order to join.

The typical club has 20 to 30 members who meet once a week for about two hours. Typical meetings might consist of:

• A short business session in which members practice and learn parliamentary procedure.
• A Table Topics session, giving members the opportunity to participate in impromptu speech situations.
• Prepared speeches from several of the club members, based on projects from the Communication and Leadership manuals.
• An evaluation session, during which each speaker is provided with valuable feedback regarding the strengths of their presentation and ideas for potential improvements.
• A critique of the evaluations and of the meeting as a whole by a general evaluator.

In addition to speaking, each member will have the opportunity to serve in several roles during the meetings, which are rotated from week to week.

Toastmasters International is a non-profit organization governed by a Board of Directors elected by the membership. TI was formed in 1924 in Santa Ana, California. For further information, contact the world headquarters of Toastmasters International.

This synopsis of TI is included in these pages as a service to our readers.

1500 South Priest Drive
Tempe, AZ 85281
602-968-2552
Fax 602-968-0911

For the person who desires to make professional speaking a serious endeavor, there is one organization with more services and answers than any other source: the National Speakers Association (NSA). This association was formed in 1973 by a handful of professional speakers who wished to unite and develop the profession. The acknowledged founder of NSA is Cavett Robert, also a member of Speakers Roundtable. NSA's first president was SR member Bill Gove.

NSA has grown to over 3,500 members worldwide with 35 chapters and its own international conference center. The annual meeting of NSA regularly draws nearly 2,000 attendees for five days of more than 200 separate events. Each quarter, there are special labs held at the International Center for Professional Speaking focusing on one of the core competencies of speaking. Two winter conventions are held, one on each side of the U.S. Additionally, members have access to *Professional Speaker* magazine, tapes of past conventions, videos, and the monthly "Voices of Experience" audio series.

NSA gives the following awards and designations:

Certified Speaking Professional (CSP): An earned designation requiring a certain number of clients, professional speeches, and a balanced, thorough professional education.

Council of Peers Award of Excellence (CPAE): An award for platform excellence. Only five CPAEs are awarded each year, and they are selected from nominations by existing CPAEs.

The Cavett Award: NSA's most cherished award. Presented annually to the member whose accomplishments over the years have reflected outstanding credit, respect, honor, and admiration on the profession of speaking. Named for the man whose example inspired the award—NSA Chairman Emeritus Cavett Robert, CSP, CPAE.

The mission of the National Speakers Association is to advance the standard of excellence in the profession of speaking and to expand the use of professional speakers.

This synopsis of NSA is included in these pages as a service to our readers.